CW01024924

BREAD

Edible

Series Editor: Andrew F. Smith

EDIBLE is a revolutionary new series of books dedicated to food and drink that explores the rich history of cuisine. Each book reveals the global history and culture of one type of food or beverage.

Already published

Apple Erika Janik

Cake Nicola Humble

Caviar Nichola Fletcher

Champagne Becky Sue Epstein

Cheese Andrew Dalby

Chocolate Sarah Moss and Alexander Badenoch

Curry Colleen Taylor Sen

Dates Nawal Nasrallah

Hamburger Andrew F. Smith

Hot Dog Bruce Kraig

Ice Cream Laura B. Weiss

Lobster Elisabeth Townsend

Milk Hannah Velten

Olive Fabrizia Lanza

Pancake Ken Albala

Pie Janet Clarkson

Pizza Carol Helstosky

Potato Andrew F. Smith

Sandwich Bee Wilson

Soup Janet Clarkson

Spices Fred Czarra

Tea Helen Saberi

Whiskey Kevin R. Kosar

Bread

A Global History

William Rubel

REAKTION BOOKS

For Jane Levi

Published by Reaktion Books Ltd
33 Great Sutton Street
London EC1V 0DX, UK
www.reaktionbooks.co.uk

First published 2011

Printed and bound in China by C&C Offset Printing Co. Ltd

British Library Cataloguing in Publication Data

Rubel, William
Bread: a global history. – (Edible)
1. Bread. 2. Bread – History.
3. Cooking (Bread)
I. Title II. Series 641.8 15-DC22

ISBN 978 1 86189 854 8

Contents

Introduction 7

1 The Early History of Bread 10

2 Bread as a Social Marker 39

3 Parameters of Taste 59

4 World of Bread: An Eccentric Travelogue 80

5 Bread in the Twenty-first Century 104

Recipes 119

Glossary 133

Select Bibliography 149

Websites and Associations 151

Acknowledgements 153

Photo Acknowledgements 154

Index 155

Introduction

Flatbread, loaf bread, fried bread, bean bread, corn bread; they are all breads. Yet when asked to go to the store to buy bread for dinner, most readers of this book will pass up all types of bread except the loaf breads. There is an accepted ambiguity in the way we use the term 'bread' that lets us both recognize bread as a hugely wide classification of foodstuffs, and to think of bread for our own table as a more narrowly defined concept. When the Spanish encountered the flat maize tortilla of Mexico they immediately recognized it as the bread of the local inhabitants. On the other hand, they also did not classify it as bread. To this day the Mexican bakery that produces tortillas, the *tortilleria*, is institutionally distinct from the bakery that produces wheat breads, the *panaderia*. Going back as much as 2,000 years people from Europe's loaf-bread cultures, when commenting on bread, have consistently acknowledged the bread of others, while insisting on the aesthetic and healthful primacy of the type of loaf bread – white – preferred by the social elite.

Throughout this book I move back and forth between a cosmopolitan reference to all breads as bread and a more narrow focus on the loaf bread as being the one true bread. This fuzziness is partly captured in how the most authoritative

English-language dictionary, the *Oxford English Dictionary* (OED), defines bread:

> A well-known article of food prepared by moistening, kneading and baking meal or flour, generally with the addition of yeast or leaven.

One way to read this definition is an admission by the lexicographer that bread is so much a cultural object that it means too many things to too many people to be pinned down. The OED is really saying that *bread* without adjectives is more the purview of the anthropologist than the lexicographer: cultural usage determines meaning, so to find the precise meaning of bread, consult the culture you want to use as the reference point.

The OED places kneading at the centre of its bread definition. While bread is certainly usually made with a kneaded dough, and as for short-hand convenience it can be helpful to put kneaded dough at the centre of its definition, there are many examples of batters that produce products that have played the functional role of kneaded breads: the many forms of the North American cornbread are an obvious example of a bread that falls outside the OED definition. The buckwheat crêpe of Brittany and the *teff ingera* of Ethiopia are pancakes that fill the role of a kneaded bread in their respective traditional culinary cultures. While this book is primarily focused on the product of kneaded dough, and specifically leavened kneaded dough, it does not impose arbitrary limits on the edges of the definition.

Bread is a concept. Bread is not harvested by farmers, it is manufactured by bakers. As an invention of culture the concept of bread can change. However, in practice, while concepts of what makes a good bread good do change with time, the core European concept of what bread is has been remarkably stable for thousands of years. Important edges to European culinary culture's definition of bread are these: kneaded or not kneaded. Lean or fatty. Salty or sweet. Dough or batter. Thick or thin. Leavened or unleavened. Big or small. In some cases singly, in others in combination, these edges mark the borders of bread and cake, of bread and flatbread, of bread and pancake, of loaf and roll. If one eliminates the overriding importance of the loaf shape, and thus accepts both leavened and unleavened flatbreads into the pantheon of daily breads, then these edges fairly universally define bread for every culture for which bread is of culinary importance, regional exceptions notwithstanding.

This book is an introduction to bread as a food and as a cultural object. Each of us who lives within a bread culture is, in fact, an expert on bread. But we don't all have the vocabulary to talk about it. One of the purposes of this book is to call attention to ways of thinking about bread that show that every loaf has a multi-layered story to tell. Bread is so twined with culture that one can start from a loaf of bread and find oneself talking about some of the largest issues of history and society. Sometimes a bread can be like a mirror reflecting back one's own image, one's own dreams, even. Why did you choose *that* particular bread for serving at a dinner for company? Bread is such a deliciously complex object that the answer to that question could be the story of one's life.

I

The Early History of Bread

Who was the first Author or Inventor of making Bread,
I will not take upon me to determine.
Thomas Moffett, 1655

We do not know who made the first breads. What we do know is that bread formed the economic and nutritional underpinnings of the civilizations that grew up in the Fertile Crescent and along the Mediterranean Sea. Bread was central to the civilization of Uruk (founded around 4000 BC) and later Mesopotamian cultures. Bread built the Old Kingdom Pyramids, it was a staple in the civilizations of ancient Greece and Rome, and bread fed most of Europe even into the nineteenth century as Britain and other European nations became the world's dominant powers. Even today, the economic power of the United States, Canada and Australia is not entirely dissociated from their vast wheat fields.

The history of bread begins in the Fertile Crescent, that part of the world centred on Iraq and including parts of adjacent countries: Afghanistan, Turkey, Kuwait, Syria, Israel, Palestine. It is here, and in particular in the lands that lie between the region's two great rivers, the Tigris and the

Cuneiform record of food supplies, including bread (top left). It seems easy to imagine breads having been stamped with cuneiform texts. Iraq, c. 3000 BC.

Euphrates, that the world's first urban cultures developed. Bread was their foundation.

But the invention of bread seems to pre-date its use as a staple food. Long before the Neolithic Revolution, when the hunters and gatherers in the Fertile Crescent made the cultural shift to farming and raising large animals (cows, goats and sheep), the peoples in the region were harvesting and eating grains from vast fields of wild barley and wheat. It is here, at least 22,500 years ago, among these wild grains, among peoples not yet tamed and settled by their domesticated plants, animals and accumulated material possessions, that recent archaeological research suggests the story of bread may begin.

Humans cannot live on raw grain; we don't have the teeth or stomachs for it. We must transform grains into food through cooking. The basic methods for making grains palatable are sprouting, fermenting, roasting, boiling and baking. Compared

Left: Free-threshing hull-less wheat was quickly adopted by ancient farmers and remains in use today. *Right*: Einkorn, an early domesticated hulled wheat, now rarely grown on a commercial scale.

with consuming grain as whole grains, grinding and baking into bread radically increases a grain's glycaemic index, releasing otherwise nutritionally unavailable carbohydrates. Bread also stores easily and is transportable, offering significant practical advantages over porridge and alcoholic fermentation for the primary use of the grain crop.

Without getting drawn into an argument about who invented what and when, and what it was that Fertile Crescent hunter-gatherers ate more of, we know from recent archaeological digs that systematic collecting and grinding of starches can be traced back thousands of years before the invention of agriculture. Starch grains from barley and possibly wheat imbedded in a grindstone found by the Sea of Galilee at the Upper Palaeolithic site of Ohalo II are between 22,500 and 23,500 years old. Dolores Piperno, the archaeologist who published the discovery, speculates that one particular grouping of burned stones at the site suggests a simple hearthstone oven.

Bread, as we now usually think of it, requires dough stiff enough to trap gases when it bakes so that a cross-section reveals an aerated crumb, not a dense mass of starch. The Fertile Crescent grains that could trap gases and were harvestable in their wild forms were barley (*Hordeum vulgare L.*) and two forms of wheat, einkorn (*Triticum monococcum L.*) and wild emmer (*Triticum dicoccoides*). We speculate that these grains were the first used for what became bread as we know it today.

Both the wild and the first domesticated forms of barley and wheat were hulled, meaning that the grain is tightly enclosed within a tenacious chaff structure called a 'glume'. After threshing to break up the stalk head, hulled wheat must be further processed to release the seed from this tightly fitting outer husk. This was usually accomplished by pounding in a mortar. Once freed of the husk the grain is cleaned by winnowing. It may be further cleaned by sifting or hand picking to remove impurities. Modern wheat and barley (though 'modern' is relative as they are many thousands of years old)

'The Threshing Floor', from Diderot's *Encyclopédie*, Paris, *c.* 1770.

A woman grinding flour, Old Kingdom Fifth Dynasty, 2465–2323 BC.

are 'free threshing'. This means that chaff freely falls away from the grain and central stalk. Once the grain is separated from the seed head by threshing it just takes winnowing and further optional cleaning to prepare grain for the miller.

Grindstones are commonly found in pre-agricultural settlements in the Fertile Crescent. They were used in pre-agricultural societies for many purposes and so their use with grain was probably merely an adaptation of an already familiar tool. Historical evidence and contemporary practice suggests that the miller was usually a woman bent over a flat rectangular stone holding a smooth-sided oblong rock in her hands. Grain was placed at the near end of the grindstone, relative to the grinder, and crushed against the large stationary flat stone in a long sweeping motion. Though the form of the grindstone changed slightly over the years, the *matate* used by women in the Mexican countryside to grind maize that was boiled in lime water into the dough called *masa* for forming into tortillas would have been recognizable and useable by Upper Paeolithic Fertile Crescent hunter-gatherers 20,000 years ago.

The grindstone, particularly the type called a 'saddle quern', is a versatile tool. Even on my first attempt to grind grain on a saddle quern I was able to produce fine meal. Depending on the quality of the stone, with harder being better, an experienced user would have been able to grind grain into any degree of fineness; from coarse cracked grain suitable for porridge to a dust suitable for fine pastry, sifting technology permitting. As the grindstone developed from being a flat stone to one that was angled, and as metal technology developed, allowing for the surface of the stone to be methodically chipped to improve its milling qualities, the milling efficiency of saddle querns improved, but at all times, with persistence, one could have produced at least some fine meal comparable with today's fine wholewheat flour. If there was adequate sifting technology it could have been separated from the coarser meal. Even before grindstone surfaces could be pointed to improve milling qualities, millers could use multiple grindstones and/or multiple *manos* – the stone they held in their hand – in order to achieve their desired results.

Fine meal and white flour, however, are two different ideas. White flour implies a concept of refinement and purity. Deriving white flour from meal is a multi-step process. Technically, when milling with stones, to get the whitest flour from the grain one must first mill in such a way as to minimize the pulverization of the bran and germ – the seed's outer coating and the granular structure that is the site of germination – and then have graduated sieves and fine cloth capable of separating the starch from the meal that is the product of milling. Einkorn, an early type of wheat, can have high levels of beta

Grinding flour in a model bakery from the tomb of Nebhepetre Mentuhotep II, from Deir el-Bahari, Egypt, 11th Dynasty, *c.* 2000 BC.

carotene, so the 'white' flour produced by einkorn can be strikingly yellow. Ancient grains also had more friable bran than modern grains so it was more difficult to keep the bran from being ground into a fine powder. Thus early breads were probably always denser than breads made with today's grains. This said, once a culture got the idea of refining flour to isolate the essence of the grain the elites could have had flour that was substantively purer than that of almost everyone else.

Both fine meal and white flour involve a greater expenditure of time than do coarse meals. White flour is inherently wasteful as all of the bran and germ must be sifted out of the meal for the flour to be truly white. Cheap white flour did not become available until the nineteenth-century industrial revolution brought together higher grain yields and steel roller mills. Prior to industrialization white flour had always represented a clear case of conspicuous consumption. In modern milling systems white flour is achieved with the removal of 25 per cent of the grain by weight. In pre-industrial milling systems 50 per cent of the grain, or much more, might have been sifted away to achieve white flour, this in the context of agricultural systems that often failed to adequately feed the local populations. It is thus probably safe to infer that in any socially striated society with the concept of white flour, prior to modern times food scarcity virtually dictated that the consumption of white bread was reserved for the elites. They were the only ones who could afford effectively to waste a substantial portion of the grain that went to make up their bread.

The three primary leavening systems for bread are those based on the diffusion of steam within thin dough exposed to high heat, the spontaneous fermentation of dough by lactobacilli (sourdough) and the purposeful introduction of yeast, which for millennia has meant *Saccharomyces cerevisiae* obtained by the baker from the brewer. All three systems can be applied to flatbreads but only leavening with sourdough and yeast is effective with loaf breads.

Sourdough starters were and are usually obtained through the spontaneous fermentation of a batter or dough that is kept in a warm place for half a day up to a few days. Since patience is the only technology required to create a dough that is sour this is a leavening system that was well within the compass of the first bread bakers. Once one has a sour dough, then dough held back from one batch can be used to inoculate the next. Sourdough cultures can be shared and therefore the technology is easy to disseminate. The open question with respect to ancient breads is what the flora of beer fermentation were like, and what that would have contributed to bread. Delwen Samuel's archaeobotanical work with ancient Egyptian beer suggests that before *S. cerevisiae* became the dominant fermenting agent the flora of beer fermentation were similar to sourdough bread cultures – the primary agents of fermentation were bacteria, not yeast. Thus what ancient Egyptian bakers might have obtained from brewers would probably have produced a bread similar to one made with a sourdough starter.

At some point, for reasons we may never learn, *S. cerevisiae*, which seems to have been first used to make wine and sake, was selected for the task of fermenting beer and, from then until the later nineteenth century, yeast was usually obtained by the baker from the brewer in the form of sediment thrown off in the production of ale. Yeast-leavened bread thus depended on the production of alcohol. The archaeological record, historic texts and ethnographic record all suggest that brewing and baking were often allied activities, often even sharing utensils such as mixing bowls. To answer the question of who used what type of leaven when and where, I think solid working premises are these: where there is warmth there is sourdough; where there is beer there is a ready source of grain-friendly fermenting flora; where there are humans there is ingenuity.

The history of bread is bedevilled by the problem of macro and micro analysis, and this problem is exacerbated by the limited data from early historical periods. On a macro level, once we know the grains that were available and the technologies for grinding, sifting and baking we can say something general about what breads were possible with a reasonable degree of certainty. But at the micro level, what precise loaves each social group in that culture might have put on their table, and what they might have thought of these breads, is largely impossible to know from most periods in history and particularly from the ancient past. The more detail one seeks regarding a loaf of bread, the more fantasy must be in the answer. At the level of recipe, how can we know what any baker baked?

Still it is worth asking what the breads of the Fertile Crescent's hunter-gatherers might have been like, because this leads to larger questions about who they were and who we are. A campfire seems to be a rough heating source for cooking and baking to those of us more used to gas and electric kitchen ranges, but in fact the campfire offers a wide range of baking options: the hot ashes can be managed to operate as an infinitely nuanced oven for baking breads in different heat gradients as the recipe requires; the embers can be utilized as a griddle for direct baking on short-lived intense heat and, after sweeping the fire away, the now exposed hot ground offers a somewhat less intense heat than embers, but the heat is more sustained.

The key concept for both early milling and baking technologies is that primitive tools do not need to imply primitive results. Exquisitely carved objects and elegant paintings by societies tens of thousands of years before the invention of grain agriculture attest to the essentially unlimited possibilities for bread-making in the context of the earliest gatherers of grains. Bread dough is plastic and easily mouldable into sculpted shapes. As modern Sardinian Easter breads suggest, these sculpted breads can be finely detailed. Early first breads could have been figurines, works of art, homages to deities, presents for lovers, toys for children. There also could easily have been flatbreads for general consumption and complexly braided sour leavened rolls. It is unlikely that bread was a staple food in this earliest possible period in its history. But that does not mean no bread tradition, or that they hadn't thought of bread forms that we don't have.

Bread is ephemeral. Few loaves are preserved from the past – even from the recent past. All we can do is speculate on what they might have been like. As a matter of philosophy, or research method, rather than focus on what the crudest breads might have been and assume our forbears achieved only the lowest common denominator, I think to discern cultural nuance it is potentially more fruitful to speculate about what the ingenuity and passion of eccentric individuals might

have achieved with bread dough. Might there have been traditions of artist-bakers in the pre- and post-agricultural period
and, if so, what might their breads have looked like? Much
later, as we enter recorded history with the civilizations of
the Fertile Crescent and ancient Egypt and are confronted with
monolithic buildings and elaborate levels of material culture,
I think it appropriate to ask what court bakers working in the
context of complex societies under the patronage of immensely
powerful priests or kings might have achieved. Consider the
complex architectural displays made of sugar in late eighteenth-century France and England, an outpouring of creative
energy and brilliant technical mastery of sugar that one could
never imagine from our own understanding of dessert or table
decoration, as a warning to us not to limit our conceptual-
ization of the breads of the ancient world to bread as we now
understand it.

We can never know why the cultures of the Fertile Crescent gave up hunting and gathering (Adam and Eve's biblical
profession) in favour of farming (Cain's biblical profession)
and herding domesticated animals (Abel's biblical profession).
There is archaeological evidence from skeletons that people
had been healthier as hunters and gatherers and that embrac-
ing agriculture – and bread as a staple – was not the best choice
for everyone. In the late eighteenth century Jean-Jacques Rousseau postulated that the adoption of farming implied slavery.
And, certainly, between the text of the Old Testament and
traditional Jewish myths surrounding the first biblical gen-
erations, farming is not cast in a good light. Cain, the first
farmer, was the first murderer, the first to lie to his Lord, the
man responsible for the first cities, by implication built with
involuntary labour. By Jewish tradition Cain was also the
man who introduced weights and measures, a sign of distrust
between people. In the Judaeo-Christian foundation myth

Adam and Eve are expelled from the idyll of the Garden of Eden, an idealized world organized around gathering, into a world where the agricultural labour of providing themselves with bread – the creation myth's staple food – will itself be so hard that it will always be felt to be a harsh punishment. In exile from Eden (our culture's mythological explanation for the Neolithic Revolution), Adam and Eve and their descendants were cursed to earn their bread by the sweat of their brow. If you have seen subsistence farmers working fields by hand with a scratch stick or even a horse-drawn plough, or seen a wheat crop being harvested by hand scythe, you will understand what a hard life farming was and that bread, life's staple, and thus a blessing, has also from the dawn of agriculture until recent times been a curse to the subsistence farmers who lived off the grain they grew, the growing of it only being the beginning of the labour to turn it into bread.

'Neolithic' is a ponderous-sounding term, the kind of classifying term that is inherently alienating. And yet, on a camping trip, or living in an isolated valley in the countryside in a simple house growing most of one's own food and raising a few animals, one is not so far from the Neolithic life, Internet connection notwithstanding. While the few pieces of Neolithic bread that have been excavated have tended to be fairly coarse products, I don't think it reasonable to extrapolate from those few breads to all Neolithic breads. In the absence of overwhelming evidence I think we will get closer to the truth of what the range of possible Neolithic breads might have been by modelling our more refined concepts after their more complex technologies and their most beautiful artwork. If the more comfortable European Neolithic societies had expended as much imaginative thought and skill on breads, at least for festivals, as they did on their more refined artefacts such as the gold and platinum alloy dagger of around 3000 BC unearthed in 2005 near Dubovo, Bulgaria, one ought to accept highly refined baked goods as at least an imaginative possibility.

Even today the chapatti and roti of many Rajasthani villages is made from flour ground daily on a rotary hand quern, the milling technology from about the fifth to the third century BC that succeeded the saddle quern. In Rajasthan flour is milled the morning of baking, sifted through a coarse sieve, then mixed with water, kneaded and made into a thin disk that is baked on a terracotta griddle heated by cow dung until the dough is set. It is then transferred to the embers where it finishes baking. The use of the griddle is a convenience. The same results can be obtained baking the bread entirely on the embers. There is nothing in the technology of this delicious bread that couldn't have been made thousands of years ago. As for leavened loaf breads and rolls, one doesn't have to find domed bread ovens to postulate their existence. Once pottery was developed, any baker with a pot could have baked rolls or a loaf bread under a pot placed over heated ground and then surrounded with embers, a cooking method that Elizabeth David describes as a practice in England into the early twentieth century.

The Neolithic period overlaps with and then ends with urbanization. The first cities were constructed in the northern section of the Fertile Crescent; the builders of the first cities were fuelled by bread. It seems to be commonly accepted that around 3200 BC a revolution in agriculture took place in what is now southern Iraq. A system of long fields watered by a centralized irrigation system was developed that so increased agricultural production that it became possible to build up sufficient surplus grain to build cities in which tens of thousands of people could live. Surplus grain allowed for craft specialization. It supported scholars. It provided food for people so that they could do things other than grow food.

Many archaeologists consider Uruk to be the world's first city. It was built around a temple complex and may have had a population of as many as 30,000 people. It was a bread-based city. The temple organized the irrigation and farming, managed labourers, took in all the grain grown and redistributed it to the populations it controlled. The primary grain of Uruk was barley, which did better than wheat in Uruk's saline soils. The culture of Uruk supported writing. And so, along with the urbanization that bread made possible, the history of bread within the compass of history as defined by the written word begins there, too. What we learn from the literature of Uruk is that bread was at the centre of their concept of civilization. In the oldest surviving story, the Epic of Gilgamesh (c. 2000 BC), what lifts Enkidu from the level of beast to that of a civilized man is eating bread and getting drunk. The association

Neo-Assyrian flood tablet relating part of the Epic of Gilgamesh, a story in which bread figures prominently. Nineveh, Iraq, 7th century BC.

Cuneiform tablet
recording barley
rations paid by
the temple of the
goddess Bau from
Tello (ancient Girsu),
Iraq, *c.* 2350–2200 BC.

of bread and alcohol was reinforced through religions cere-
monies. Reports on the offerings made to deities in the Ur
III period (3100–2900 BC) often began, 'The bread looks nice,
the beer tastes good.' As I am writing about bread – not religion – I refer again to the fact that where there is beer (even
if it is different from our own sort) there is easy access to
leavening, so one can imagine leavened loaves as a possibility
for the deities. I think it is for the poet-baker working with
period technologies, perhaps even more than the archaeologist, to find a range of bread possibilities to offer to the deities
of Ur.

Uruk was just a beginning. The forces of urbanization
were gathering in parallel in the southern portion of the
Fertile Crescent, that of the Nile river valley. The civilizations
of Mesopotamia grew to ever greater levels of material prosperity. In later periods palaces included specialized rooms for
bread production: the milling room in the second-millenium
palace at Ebla permitted at least fifteen millers to work at the
same time. Thanks to the world of Jean Bottero, a French

scholar who has done extensive work on the Yale University Sumerian culinary texts, we know that breads were an integral part of elaborate court meals and that more generally bread was associated with good fortune, plenty and prosperity. This verse from the eleventh tablet of the Epic of Gilgamesh illustrates the point:

> He will bring to you a harvest of wealth,
> in the morning he will let loaves of bread shower down,
> and in the evening a rain of wheat!

Unfortunately, we have no recipes and no images of Sumerian court breads, only the sense that the range of barley and wheat breads was fantastically expansive, as one would expect from a court with a complex and refined material culture. Breads were baked on the sidewalls of tandoor-style

Panel of Ashurnasirpal II, 883–859 BC. Imagine elegant barley or wheat crackers stamped with elaborate images like this one, like German gingerbreads.

ovens and on the floor of domed ovens. There was a mix of leavened and leavened breads, breads that were baked and fried and breads mixed with fruits, oils and honey. A distinctive feature of the bread culture compared with ours was the apparent prevalence of moulded breads. A great many bread moulds have been excavated, including moulds that either impressed a pattern or image onto the underside of the bread or baked the bread into a shape, like that of a fish. The practical work has yet to be done with period technologies, artefacts and texts to imagine in real dough what Mesopotamian breads might have been like. The texts are limited; the timelines long. As clay and dense dough would take the same kind of inscription, I imagine that there might have been breads, or at least crackers, covered in writing: prayers, divination, stories. Keeping in mind that unique European flowering of the art of sugar sculpture in the eighteenth century and the bas-reliefs at Nimrod commissioned by Ashurnasirpal II (c. 883–859 BC), might not his court baker have constructed in bread elaborate

Saber Hassan El Sharkawi, age fourteen, *Baking Bread at Home*, Egypt, c. 1980.

bas-reliefs to line the walls of a tent on one of the king's hunting expeditions?

In ancient Egypt, as in the civilizations of the Fertile Crescent, bread and beer were often paired, both being offered to the deities, and both staples of daily life. To say bread was the staple food is not to suggest that there might not have been large groups of the poor who ate porridge or pulses as their staple – only that the culture itself saw bread as its staple and anyone who could afford it ate it in quantity. While beer has been dropped from today's typical Egyptian diet, bread remains a substantial source of calories for a large proportion of the Egyptian population.

The bread-related artefacts that we have from ancient Egypt are remarkable in both quantity and quality of detail. There are more bread-related artifices from Ancient Egypt than from any period up to modern times. Wooden models of bakeries have survived so we know exactly how bakeries were furnished and staffed; ruins of production bakeries have been excavated; there are many hieroglyphic bread texts and bread has been found in the stomachs of un-mummified remains; and the back rooms of many museums contain desiccated breads that were left as tomb offerings. And yet what we don't have are recipes or even the limited context for bread within the palace kitchen that we get from the Yale Sumerian culinary texts. Even though there are so many paintings – braided breads, breads shaped as animals, pyramidal breads, flat-breads, multi-kilo moulded conical breads and much more besides (including those actual desiccated breads) – one can study the vast amount of information about bread from ancient Egypt and find little more than ideas searching for form. Some experimental archaeologists have begun milling flour using emmer and period tools and getting their hands wet with dough but, despite the work that has been done on the history of ancient Egypt, bread, which was in so many ways at the centre of that life, remains an enigma.

Emmer, *Triticum dicoccum* and, it seems to a much lesser extent, barley were the most important bread grains used in Egypt up to the Ptolemaic period, around 300 BC, when the hard wheat species grown today – a form of free-threshing wheat, *T. durum* – replaced emmer. This both is and isn't helpful for anyone trying to recreate ancient Egyptian breads. There would have been innumerable landraces of both barley and emmer. In the context of a civilization that so prized the aesthetics of material objects, and for whom bread was such an

Bakers mixing and kneading dough and filling bread moulds. Painting in the tomb of Qenamun, Sheikh Abd el-Qurna, West Thebes, Egypt. New Kingdom, 18th Dynasty, 1550–1295 BC.

Loaf of tomb
bread from
Deir el-Bahari,
Thebes, Egypt,
New Kingdom,
c. 1500 BC.

important foodstuff, it seems safe to assume that elite bakers
would have commanded emmer from farms that produced a
premium product, however that was defined. Literally thousands of years of selection would have gone into some of
those landraces, and what was considered 'best' in a bread will
undoubtedly have changed innumerable times over the course
of Egyptian history.

There is a current romance with the idea of ancient Egyptian sourdough. One can even buy a sourdough culture over
the Internet that is romantically linked with Giza. Whether
ancient Egypt, awash in beer, had a respect for spontaneous
sourdough cultures over the cultures that could be obtained
from the brewer, whatever its ratio of bacteria to yeast, I
cannot say, but I would guess that high-status Egyptians surrounded by so much material wealth would have demanded
the best, however defined.

The most intriguing Egyptian breads are the ones that
we can actually see: the roll-sized tomb loaves that survived in
desiccated form. Many of these breads are in geometric shapes,

often triangular, but whatever the shape they are usually compact, and never seem to exhibit the obvious effects of expansion of the dough while baking. They often include pieces of bran, suggesting a dense dough made with wholegrain flour. Shape and control of the bread's form throughout baking seem to be important aspects of the baker's concept for these breads. Perhaps the colour of the finished bread was important. Perhaps some were glazed and coloured so they would glow in the desert sun. How these particular breads, usually associated with elite tombs, often made with coarse flour, even flour that contained chaff and was contaminated with sand, related to breads that people ate is unknown. As the experimental archaeologist Delwen Samuel points out, virtually no breads have been excavated from settlements.

The Egyptian language itself contains tantalizing hints of breads that can be found in dictionaries of hieroglyphics, though we lack a social context for the breads mentioned. *Ta hari* is 'the bread from under', a reference that usually denotes something to do with excrement, but whether this refers to shape, colour, form, technique or something else is hard to know, and it is equally difficult to interpret 'tender' or 'effeminate' bread. Other names refer to ingredients, probably straightforward enough when berries are mentioned, but how should we understand 'blood bread'? Whether that was a bread made with blood, glazed with blood or to be dipped in blood, or a bread that had some kind of symbolic relationship with blood, is so far unanswerable, quite apart from questions of recipe and use.

Greece rose in power as Egyptian power declined. We don't have the extensive array of bread artefacts from ancient Greece that we have from Egypt, but we have literary evocations of bread in stories we still read. From the *Odyssey* we learn that flour was milled daily for the residents of Odysseus' palace.

Women probably grinding grain with flautist, Thebes, Greece, *c.* 525–475 BC.

When he dined as a guest we learn that bread was passed to him in baskets, thus tying the twenty-first-century waiter's offering of a dinner roll with a custom and a gesture from 3,000 years ago. Greek art, in particular Greek sculpture, exerts an influence on our artistic tradition that the works of ancient Egypt don't. From ancient Greece we have many lovely little sketches of daily life made in terracotta, including figurines of bakers, almost always personable little sculptures that seem to capture the intimacy of a moment frozen in time. Just a few centimetres high, many depict a baker sitting in front of an oven that is open in front and can either be heated from below or from a fire within the oven, frequently filled with rolls and with a basket at the baker's feet. In the Louvre in Paris there is a figurine that conveys the feeling of a snapshot. It depicts women standing at a worktable, probably grinding flour while a flautist plays a song to entertain them. From this we can imagine the shade of a fig tree, children running around, dogs barking, birds singing, the melody of the flute playing over the sound of rhythmic grinding and later the smell of loaves baking in the dry Greek air.

While it is still a specialist's game to work out what the range of Ancient Greek breads might have been like, with a thorough review of the archaeology, art, literature and ethnography, plus quite a lot of imagination, I think one could make a stab at *eskharites*, meaning brazier-baked; *bolitinos artos* or mushroom-shaped; *semidalites*, *krithinos artos* and *khondrite*, breads named after the grains used to make them, durum, barley and emmer; *katharos artos*, white bread, and the contrasting *autopyros artos*, wholemeal bread.

Aspects of Egyptian, Greek and Roman culture began to merge towards the end of the ancient period as Greece extended its influence to Egypt, followed by Rome building an empire that encompassed Greece and North Africa, among its many conquests. It is from this period that we find one of the first descriptions of a bread that feels viscerally real. It is found in Athenaeus' (AD 170–230) food-related text *Deipnosophistae*. The book is built out of a series of dialogues between diners. There may be a bit of the tall tale in this discussion of barley bread but even so I think the passage is important. Athenaeus describes a simple meal in which a chaff-filled barley bread is featured, a bread perhaps not dissimilar to an Egyptian tomb bread. One of the diners, Poliochus, says:

> Both of us broke a bit of black barley bread, with chaff mixed in the kneading twice a day, and had a few figs; sometimes, too, there would be a braised mushroom, and if there were a little dew we'd catch a snail, or we'd have some native vegetables or crushed olive, and some wine to drink of dubious quality.

In response Antiphanes offers his own barley bread story. Of another 'barley bread bristling with chaff' he explains that when he was eating this coarse bread he was living a 'mode

Guercino, *St Paul the Hermit*, c. 1620–60.

of life, without heat, without excitement'. In other words, Poliochus and Antiphanes ate (or for purposes of argument boasted of eating) an exceedingly coarse barley bread apparently in the context of adventures, even if acetic ones. Those who had no choice but to eat coarse bread would presumably not have thought of it in so positive a light. I think we have here an early hint of how the Christian religion would use coarse breads to denote saintliness. Early Christian hermits are recorded as eating coarse brown breads as part of their programmes of spiritual cleansing. Many paintings depict St Paul the Hermit, also known as Paul of Thebes (d. *c.* 345), living in the desert and being brought bread in the beak of a raven. The paintings customarily depict a dark bread; one can guess a black rye or brown wheat bread. Many a hermit will have punished his body with the coarsest breads in pursuit of a mode of life without heat or excitement.

Rome was the last of the great early Western civilizations. Thanks to the tragedy of Vesuvius' eruption in AD 79, besides

Excavating a bakery in Pompeii with carbonized bread still in the oven, *c.* 1860.

charred loaves we can see via a well-preserved wall painting a late Roman bakery with golden-hued loaves stacked on shelves behind the counter – a style of display familiar today. From the painting it seems clear that these are leavened breads. Whether made of bread wheat or of durum flour like the *pane di Altamura* of today's Apulia, I think it safe to infer that we would find the heft of the breads familiar, as we would the crunch of the crust between our teeth and the feel and taste of the crumb in our mouth. The breads in the painting feel so familiar that that they cast a glow both forwards and backwards in time. Ultimately, loaf breads are loaf breads and the chemistry of dough is fixed. What they ate then and what we eat now need not have been different at all. So what were the breads like in the vast geographic expanse of Roman Europe? What can be said in general is this: the poor ate dense wholegrain breads and breads made of pulses, peas and fava beans, acorns, chestnuts or whatever they could scrounge that was nutritious, filling and cheap. They baked their breads in the ashes of their fires, on griddles and under clay pots around which embers were placed, and in what we call Dutch ovens, pots that could be heated by embers both under the pot and on its lid. As one moved up the social ladder the breads came to be more like the breads we know today and were more likely to be baked in domed, wood-fired bread ovens – the same technology urban elite artisan bakers use today (most famously the ovens of the Poilâne bakery in Paris). Breads were baked with all the bread flours we know: bread wheat, durum, barley and rye, with the even more ancient varieties of hulled wheat largely persisting as remnant crops in isolated communities. Wheat ruled amongst the elite. There were white breads and also a range of enriched breads, made with olive oil, olives, figs and lardoons, and it is also safe to speculate that, climate being favourable, there were breads enriched with Northern Europe's staples of milk, butter and eggs. Athenaeus describes a bread with a light and airy crumb that sounds very like the ciabatta that is so popular today – a bread made with a dough so hydrated that when first mixed it is a batter.

Preserved carbonized bread excavated from a baker's oven in Pompeii, baked 24 August, AD 79.

Willem van Herp the Elder, *St Anthony of Padua Distributing Bread*, c. 1662.

In the sixteenth and seventeenth centuries writers who discussed bread in health manuals, like Thomas Cogan or Thomas Tyron, referred to Roman classifications in describing the flour and breads of their own period. For example, Thomas explains that the English white wheat 'manchet' was the *Panis siliginius* of Rome, thus at least rhetorically linking the bread back some 1,200 years. Other ideas about bread from the Graeco-Roman world were transferred into our modern culture through the writings of the Greek physician Galen, the most influential European medical writer up to the early modern era. In many ways what Galen and his later interpreters wrote about bread is more or less what we, as a culture, think today. White bread was favoured over bran breads, with the exception of the occasional need for bulk to help pass too compacted a stool. Loaf breads were favoured over flatbreads. Wheat was favoured over all other grains. Medical reasons were articulated for these preferences, which were probably not just coincidentally aligned with what was

Jacob Meydenbach, hand-coloured woodcut of a woman preparing loaves of bread, illustration from *Hortus Sanitatis* (1491).

by then already long historic precedent – the rich preferred light, white, wheat breads to dense, dark, bran-filled ones.

Bread is at the centre of Christianity, a religion formed out of Graeco-Roman culture and very much present in our own time. To this day, in one form or another, most Christian sects bring bread into their church and while they disagree on the precise interpretation, concepts of bread and the body of Christ are central to Christianity. From the very beginning of bread's history it seems that bread has been at the centre of both religious and secular life for the peoples who depended on it for sustenance. Bread has always meant more than just something to eat, so I'd like to close this first chapter in a history of bread with a sentiment expressed by Alexander Pope more than 1,000 years after the fall of Rome. Allowing for different conceptions of the role of deities in the world, like the different breads on our tables, this verse from Pope's 'The Universal Prayer' (1738) would have been understood by every culture that put bread at the centre of theirs.

> This day be bread and peace my lot;
> All else beneath the sun,
> Thou know'st it best bestow'd or not,
> And let thy will be done.

2
Bread as a Social Marker

Such was the size, O master, of the nastus,
A large white loaf. It was so deep, its top
Rose like a tower quite above its basket.
Its smell, when that the top was lifted up,
Rose up, a fragrance not unmix'd with honey
Most grateful to our nostrils, still being hot.
Nicostratus, son of Aristophanes, *c.* 370 BC, in Athenaeus,
The Deipnosophists, c. AD 200

White bread! So light! So pure! So attractive! But also, up to the industrialization of milling in the nineteenth century, so expensive. For most of Europe's history, even if farmers grew grain, few had the reliable supply of excess wheat that white flour implied. In fact, comparatively few had either the farm-land capable of producing healthy stands of pure wheat or the money to buy white wheat breads if they didn't have the land. As a rule, in human cultures if something is desirable yet out of bounds, then possessing that thing suggests a high social status.

There are two large-scale arcs that move breads over time, both of which relate to bread as a social marker. The first of these arcs, and the most powerful, is the near universal rejection of the breads of poverty by virtually everyone who could afford the alternative. The second arc, more fine-grained, is that of fashion. In this chapter, I focus on the larger of these two arcs, the rejection by elite diners of the breads of the poor. It is a major subject of this book that this rejection has ancient roots and is the primary dynamic that drives most modern tastes in bread, including the ways in which most rye and brown breads are now formulated.

This chapter focuses on breads of poverty from a period when white-as-snow loaves were largely the purview of those who lived lives of conspicuous consumption. As an example, only a white loaf made with the finest flour will open in the oven like a flower, like the bread in Lubin Baugin's *Still-life with Chessboard* (1630), a painting that depicts, among other things, the vanities of life. In contrast to seductive white rolls, the honest peasants in the Le Nain brothers' seventeenth-century paintings pose around large loaves of rye bread. One

Lubin Baugin, *Still-life with Chessboard*, 1630.

of the first signs of the industrial revolution in eighteenth-century England was that increasing numbers of small farmers and farm workers lost 'their rye teeth', as a farm hand explained when describing his preference for wheat breads to a British government agricultural commission in 1795. Miss Tox, a pathetic sycophant in Charles Dickens's *Dombey and Son* (1848), well aware that the bread on one's table said something about one's social position, demonstrates her hopeless pretensions by eating French rolls for breakfast, and 'rasped' ones at that, aping the bread of her betters and thus making a further fool of herself.

As food, we can reduce bread to its nutritional components – so much protein, so much carbohydrate, so many calories per bite. The story of bread as food is a much less interesting story than the story of bread as a social marker. The nutritional analysis of bread is fundamentally reductionist; it flattens differences between loaves. An example: in the Anglo-American bread culture of today a soft plastic-wrapped industrially produced white bread that one takes off a grocery shelf and puts into one's shopping basket is culturally distinct from a white crusty artisan-produced loaf that is pulled off a shelf by a clerk in a bakery, put into a paper bag and then handed to you over a counter. Yet nutritionally there is no meaningful difference between them. Although many breads are nutritionally fungible, culturally they are rarely interchangeable. In the most extreme difference, the bread from the poorer man's table is very likely to look out of place on the rich man's table, even now. What does *good*, *better* and *best* bread mean, who makes the rules and why and how do we get caught up in them? More personally, why do I like the bread I like?

It is through culture that we pass on world-views into the distant future. The love of fine wheat breads is one of the preferences that seems to be universal: it is no accident that in terms of acreage wheat is the single biggest agricultural crop in the world, nor that most of it is ground into white flour. In times less rich in material culture, moving out of the breads of poverty into the more refined wheat-centred breads of the social elites was often the first use of increasing personal wealth. In eighteenth-century France this became a problem for the *ancien régime* because it was sometimes difficult for the government to supply Paris with sufficient wheat to feed the population's increasing appetite for white bread given the loss of grain volume inherent in the production of white flour. More recently, the increasing affluence of Russia, the former Soviet Union and its former client states is matched with a decline in the consumption of rye breads, demonstrating that rising affluence and the rejection of rye is a dynamic still working today.

Bread depicted in European paintings from the sixteenth to the eighteenth centuries often illustrates the association between white breads and luxury and brown breads and poverty. Today, an artist using bread to illustrate social status in a British or American household might depict an affluent family at the table with a loaf of crusty *pain de campagne* or a ciabatta and a poor family with a loaf of industrially produced pre-sliced bread. One way to simplify the difference between the breads of the rich and poor, now and in the past, is that the poor always eat the cheaper breads. Today, that means mass-produced white bread. But looking at contemporary bread culture at a distance, blurring the differences we see between wheat breads, what seems clear is that in millennial terms, a communal dream of eating the bread of kings has been realized.

The early modern period (1500–1800) is the first era in which we find reproducible bread recipes. It is also the period just before the Industrial Revolution turns the world upside

Louis Le Nain, *The Happy Family, or the Return of Baptism*, 1642.

down. Though distant from us, we still relate to early modern writing, art, music and literature. The US Supreme Court studies the runes of an eighteenth-century constitution. Many of the breads we like today – the standard white sandwich loaf, baguette-style breads and rolls, brioche and *pain de campagne* – can be directly traced to this period. Though now breads for all of us, at the time these were luxury breads available to a comparative few. For the bulk of Europe (I discuss some exceptions to this in chapter Four under my discussion of the breads of Germany) and for all of its former colonies, the denseness and darkness that characterized the poverty breads of the early modern period, including both wholegrain wheat breads and 100 per cent rye breads, are precisely the qualities that most bakers strive to avoid in their breads.

In England, well into the 1600s, breads for horses, known as horse-breads, were widely sold. Horse-breads were flatbreads made with bran stuck together with rye flour, also sometimes containing chaff, straw and the waste from the bakery floor. These breads were fed to horses to enable them to do strenuous work like pulling carts and trotting long distances. The retail price of horse-breads was regulated by a statute called the Assize for Bread, the same statute that regulated the price of 'man's bread'. However, it seems that horse-bread, at least the less chaff-filled variety, was sometimes eaten by the poor, as it was one third of the price of the cheapest wholegrain loaf. Horse-bread fills the belly; there are references in eighteenth-century English comic theatre to eating horse-bread when going through bad times. As a speciality bread I find horse-bread made with bran and rye (but not straw, chaff or floor sweepings) to be delicious, but you have to eat up to one kilogram (2.2 lb) a day for a few days to get a sense of what it actually felt like for this bread to be your staple food.

In one of the first modern English-language cookbooks, *The English Housewife* (1615), Gervase Markham provides a rare glimpse of bread recipes for an English estate and an almost unique example of a recipe for a bread intended for low-status farm workers, in his language the *hind servants*. Markham's 'Brown Bread' is made from flour ground from dried peas mixed with boiling water to reduce its disagreeable smell and then added to a mix of minimally sifted wheat, rye and barley flour to make a stiff dough. This is left to naturally sour in the dough trough and then baked into large loaves. It was a dense, sour and not entirely pleasant-smelling bread. The crudeness of its ingredients and the carelessness of its manufacture was in stark contrast to the white bread intended for the master's table or the slightly less refined bread intended for nearly everyone else.

One can gain further insight into this bread and its social meaning from the period's veterinary literature. Markham was

Horse-bread soured for human consumption, based on English texts, *c.* 1700.

Bread made with pea and rye flour based on proportions mentioned in the *Farming and Memorandum Book of Henry Best of Elmswell, England* (1642).

the expert on horse training in the late Elizabethan age and through his books on the subject his influence in this field extended for more than a century. In particular he was an expert on the feeding and exercise of racehorses. Markham's breads for racehorses were modelled after the white bread for the master's table. No bread he fed to racehorses was as crudely made as his brown bread for farm workers. For the racehorses he specified the finest white flour ground on the best grindstones, yeast, careful working of the dough and the flour of broad (fava) beans, not peas, as pea flour was held to be an inferior and unhealthy product. Markham's bread for racehorses is delicious. The crust of the horse-bread was chipped off because, in keeping with the medical thinking of the day, it was thought this aided digestion – something that was done for the bread of the master as well. The coarse bread served to the farm workers was served crust intact. Even in a society more used than ours to the idea of a fixed social hierarchy, it must have felt terrible to be able to see by the bread on one's table that one's food wasn't worth the trouble the master put into that of a horse.

Evidence from outside cookbook literature suggests that Markham's dense, sour, pea-adulterated brown bread was a standard bread of the rural poor. Henry Best, of Elmswell, England, in a farm memorandum book written in the 1640s describes the ingredients used by the local peasantry for their breads (which could have been made almost anywhere in northern Europe):

> Poore folkes putte usually a pecke of pease to a bushell of Rye, and some againe two peckes of pease to a fundell of Maseldine [maslin], and say that these make hearty bread.

Hearty is meant in the sense of nourishing – and in the concept of the time, it means nourishing for a labourer. These breads were thought injurious to the health of the more sedentary elite. The first recipe, a peck of pea flour to a bushel of rye, is a ratio of 1:4 pea to rye.

Meal was refined into flour through sifting, on a gradient from unsifted meal to the whitest white flour. Bread prices were regulated. The English bread laws were typical: bakers worked under price controls, their profit per loaf was fixed and it was independent of the price of grain. From the thirteenth to the eighteenth century, all breads in bakeries were subject to the Assize for Bread, thus the locus for bread creativity was the private baker. Breads were sold for fixed prices: one penny, half a penny, a quarter penny. Since the price of the loaf never changed – not for hundreds of years – what changed with the price of wheat was the size of the loaf you bought. Thus when wheat was dear your penny got you a smaller loaf than when it was cheap. But whatever the price of wheat, on a given day you could buy a white bread for a penny or a wholewheat loaf for a penny or any number of breads whose refinement was between that of wholewheat and white. As one moved up (and down) the social ladder one bought smaller or bigger loaves as one got closer to (or farther away) from the ideal of a white loaf.

In the European bread hierarchy a loaf bread, however constructed, stood above all forms of flatbreads, including ash cakes (small flatbreads baked in hot ashes), griddle-baked flatbreads, pancakes and boiled grains or porridge. Millet's evocative painting *Les Glaneuses* (1857) depicts women gleaning wheat fields collecting racemes of wheat into posy-like groupings that would have been good for nothing more than boiled grains or porridge. This is in marked contrast to all those lovely aromatic white loaves one can imagine being made from the stacks of wheat sheaves in the painting's background.

Barley flatbread from a stereo card, *c.* 1910.

Alfred Walter Bayes, *Baking Oatcakes, Britain, c.* 1880, etching.

While loaf breads are indisputably the primary breads of European cuisine, there were areas in Europe where travellers would have been more likely to encounter flatbreads than loaf breads. Samuel Johnson famously pointed this out in his dictionary by giving the definition of oats as 'A grain, which in England is generally given to horses, but in Scotland supports the people.' Oatcakes were, in fact, not just a food for eighteenth-century Scots, as Johnson suggested: they were also eaten in Scandinavia and northern England, among other regions. There is an insightful interchange in Charlotte Brontë's *Shirley* (1849) in which the French tutor rejects a meal of milk and 'Yorkshire oat-cakes' even though they were the bread of the household for whom 'the husky oat-cake was from custom suave as manna'. Though usually poor people's food, in certain regions the local fare was sometimes taken up by the more affluent, as in the household described by Brontë.

If one looks carefully one can find bits and pieces of the European flatbread tradition that have survived into the twenty-first century. The most obvious examples are industrially produced flatbreads such as Scottish oatcakes, widely available in the UK, various Scandinavian crisp rye breads such as Swedish *knäckebröd*, sold internationally, and the soft pitta-like *piadina* originally from the Romagna region and now sold throughout Italy.

In Italy, especially, one sees subsistence flatbreads elevated to tourist attractions. For example, in the mountains above Modena the *crescentine*, a flatbread traditionally baked between *tigelle*, tiles heated in the embers of the fireplace, is featured in roadside restaurants that scream TIGELLE from over-sized signs. However, the modern restaurant version is baked on thermostatically controlled electric griddles from recipes that owe more to American quick breads than the breads of the region. This example highlights the perils of inferring from a traditional name that one is actually eating a traditional food as it was known when it was central to the local diet.

The websites of industrial Italian manufacturers of *piadina* suggest using them as wraps, open-faced sandwiches, bun-like sandwiches, sandwiches in which the bread is folded in half, and as the base for pizza. While flatbreads tend not to

Left: Griddle breads prepared by the Historical Cooking Guild of the Catawba Valley at James Polk House, Charlotte, North Carolina, 2003. *Right*: Sardinian *pane carasau*, a traditional flatbread.

be served as the bread for the main course in European-style meals they now often have a role in informal lunches and as part of the first course. Thus the flatbreads of Europe's previous endemic poverty have been re-imagined in the context of our present-day prosperity.

The poorer the European region, the more likely it is that one can still glimpse the tail end of the European flatbread tradition in situ, though today's wealth has tended to homogenize the product. The *pane carasau* of Sardinia is eaten locally but now it is made from fine semolina, while even 50 years ago it was only the village priest and the teacher whose bread was made with this grade of flour; everyone else ate a *pane carasau* made from a less refined flour, and in the more distant past sometimes barley flour. Sardinia's sourdough starters were famous but now the breads are made with yeast. The modern version of the bread is probably less flavourful, if more refined, than most of its historic antecedents. When we look at what seem to be still-living European flatbread traditions, such as the *yufka* of Cappadocia in Greece or the Balkan *lepinja*, it is worth noting that before ultra-refined flour was cheap these breads were probably very different from those we see today.

Pancakes are a form of flatbread and in some regions of Europe pancakes functioned as a staple bread, notably the French crêpe and the Russian blini. Even while they were a staple food of endemic poverty, the crêpe and the blini escaped their sour-batter buckwheat and rye antecedents to find themselves embraced by elite diners. One of the oft-repeated foundation stories for the luxury dessert *crêpes Suzette* is that it was developed in honour of the Prince of Wales in 1895 by the chef Henri Charpentier. While this claim may not necessarily be true, it does firmly place what was the lowly crêpe, now made with white wheat flour enriched with cream and eggs, at the best tables of the belle époque. Yeast-leavened white flour blini with caviar is still a staple of high-end hors d'oeuvres.

Left: Jadaviga, a country woman making blini, near Labanoros, Lithuania, 1992. *Right*: Roma woman with platter of crêpes for her family. Deva, Romania, 2004.

A characteristic of European flatbreads was that they were leavened with sourdough. This is true of the staple buckwheat crêpe of Brittany. Sour, dark and unenriched, it is at the opposite extreme from the cultural ideal of a lovely, light, aromatic white loaf. Relative wealth finally came to Brittany in the twentieth century. The bakeries of Brittany are now like those in the rest of France. People eat wheat bread, mostly white, and, however celebrated the *galette de sarrasin* may be at festivals, for all practical purposes the sour buckwheat crêpe was rejected by the people of Brittany in favour of white loaf breads as soon as they could afford to do so. Flatbreads are a footnote to European bread history.

No story that involves people is ever simple. There are notable exceptions to the general flight to white loaf breads as Europeans acquired the trappings of prosperity but all involve a culture re-evaluating bread and its meaning and usually also modifying the peasant recipe to make the bread more like white bread. There are many early modern references to the superior flavour and keeping qualities of a bread that included some rye, but the more common focus on brown breads among those who could afford white bread seems to have been, as it is today, on the benefits bran has on regulating bowel movements and, as now, on its nutritional content. In pre-modern conceptions of nutrition branny bread was thought to be slimming. There have always been eccentrics with strong personalities who ate what they liked. William Ellis, a mid-eighteenth century agricultural writer, describes a duchess who only served wholemeal bread. But for most wealthy people brown breads were not served at tables laden with silver and Sèvres porcelain. When brown breads were served in affluent homes, it was at the less formal family meals.

Even in the eighteenth century in Westphalia the crudest and densest of all black breads – Westphalian pumpernickel –

was served at the best tables sliced thinly with butter. Today a tamer version of what was a coal-black bread of dirt-poor peasants is sold internationally pre-sliced in plastic wrappers explicitly for hors d'oeuvres – in other words as a taste rather than as a food. Scottish oatcakes and the plentiful examples of German and other northern European rye breads prospering in the midst of plenty are examples of breads that have been imbued with cultural meaning to serve as anchors for group identity. Even so, as with the Sardinian *pane carasau* mentioned earlier, the bread celebrated today is likely to be less dense or otherwise more refined than the poverty breads from which they are derived.

Historically, the whitest loaves were always smaller than other loaves. The highest-status breads of all were baked in the form of rolls, a form one can think of as a labour-intensive personal loaf. White breads were formulated to be 'light'. The higher-status the bread the 'lighter' it had to be, meaning it

Rye bread stamped with a pattern.

had to have both distinct air holes (though not necessarily large ones) and a soft crumb. Since there is an inverse relationship between rising time and the softness of the bread, the softest breads must be yeast-leavened because only yeast can push a dough fast enough to produce the theoretically softest crumb. The addition of some fat further softens the crumb and thus it is no surprise that the early modern French court bread, *pain à la Reine*, the queen's bread, was made with both yeast and milk. The breads identified in late eighteenth-century and early nineteenth-century French baking texts as belonging to the class of breads then known as *pain à la mode*, fashionable bread, were lightly enriched with milk or butter and leavened with yeast, but the tradition was already long established. Here is a fashionable bread, *pain à la Montoron*, published by Nicolas de Bonnefons in his cookbook *Les Delices de la compaigne* (1658).

> Take a boisseau [10 kg/22 lb] of the whitest flour one can get; make a starter with one quarter of the flour by adding two cupped handfuls of new beer yeast, or a little less if the yeast is a little old and has settled, one handful salt dissolved in warm water, and three quarts of milk; about an hour later, add the rest of the flour along with water as needed to form a soft dough; turn out the dough & set them to rise in small wooden bowls then bake; & when they have baked take them out and set them on their edges to cool; one hour should suffice for cooking.

This recipe is emblematic of the luxury loaf. It is the polar opposite of the sour-leavened pea, wheat and rye bread of Henry Best's memorandum book from the same period. It is as white as money could buy, and money could buy flour that, in the words of the English edition of *La Maison rustique* of

1616, was 'as white as snow'. Through the use of yeast, a soft dough, a fairly fast rise and a minimal amount of mixing, Bonnefons ensured that his bread would have an open crumb with a soft but not chewy texture.

Other pre-industrial bread recipes, in both England and France, include a little fat in the form of egg and/or butter. In England this was often true of the recipe for an eighteenth-century bread known as 'French bread', a bread similar to Miss Tox's French roll. This recipe by William Howard was published in 1709:

> Take one quart of Flour [roughly 500g, a little over 1 lb], three eggs, a little Barm, and a little Butter; mix them with the Flour very light, with a little new Milk warmed; then lay it by the Fire to rise; then make it into little Loaves; flour it very well, and bake it in a quick Oven.

If you eliminate the eggs this is a basic modern sandwich bread and, if baked as written, it is like today's Jewish challah. In both this and the Bonnefons recipe it is significant how little reference there is to working the dough. This was deliberate. Both of these breads rest on the cusp between bread and cake – as does the modern brioche. Minimal mixing is also a feature of industrial pre-packaged breads and, for the same reason, it makes for a soft crumb.

The recipe by Howard is on the scale of modern cookbook bread recipes. As the dough is broken up into 'little loaves' one sees that it is a recipe for rolls. Howard's French bread contains markers of conspicuous consumption. It says: we have so many eggs we can also put them into our daily bread; we have the time to make bread into little rolls or the money to pay someone to do it for us. We will eat this bread to taste it, not to live on it. In part, this bread is an ornament, like those depicted in Dutch seventeenth-century still-life paintings. Silver goes with white rolls, breads that fit in with the perfect flowers, the oysters, the linen, the reflective surfaces, the luxury of the affluent table. And I think it probable that the many breads from the ancient world that were recorded as containing enrichments such as oil and fruit communicated this same kind of message: the table on which you find this bread belongs to someone who eats bread for pleasure.

In the democratization of taste that took place in the nineteenth century, as vast numbers of the European peasantry moved into cities and moved up the social ladder, breads that had been at the top of the social ladder became quotidian. While there is a contemporary critique of the qualities of soft breads found in industrial breads, in profound ways our industrial breads incorporate the ideal of bread as it was conceived for centuries, if not millennia. One might even say that the cultural critique of so much bread as 'empty calories' is in fact its greatest triumph: in its very essence is baked the cultural marker that says 'Whoever buys this bread does not live on bread alone.'

Because of the inherent shortcuts taken in the making of industrial bread – it is made by robots; no human care, not even a touch, is expended on any one loaf – it shares the cultural marker of expediency that went with the sour-leavened loaves of poverty and the huge loaves of bread baked for the working poor. In England, depending on the era, brown breads purchased in the bakery could weigh 9–14 kg (20–30 lb), or more. The larger of the two loaves carried by the servant in Jean-Baptiste-Siméon Chardin's painting *Return from the Market* (1739) is so large and heavy the woman carrying it has to rest it on a table while she eavesdrops on the other servant's conversation with the man in the doorway. As mentioned in the context of the English baking laws, the

Pain bouilli (boiled bread), Villar d'Arène, France, 2007.

larger the loaf, the less refined the flour that was used to bake it. We can infer from its size that the large loaf is made with something other than white flour.

The place to look in one's own life for an example of bread functioning almost purely as a social marker is on the formal dinner table. Bread really doesn't have a culinary role on the modern dinner table. It is there by custom. One may be annoyed not to see it there, but it is not an integral part of the meal. The host will not think anything of it if you eat everything on your plate but don't touch the bread. The starch that is part of the meal is on the plate – it is the potato, the rice, the polenta. The more care you take in selecting the loaf, and the less is eaten, the more you can know that in your own household the bread's primary function is something other than food. The less we need it the more it is like the dinner set, and as with the dinner set, the more it can be parsed for subtle social cues. And that is the subject of the next chapter – the various aspects of bread from crust to crumb that are manipulated by the baker to serve the dual role of giving the bread its character as a food and a range of messages as a cultural object.

3
Parameters of Taste

If there is one thing more annoying than another to the baker,
it is to cut a handsome-looking loaf and to find it full of large,
unsightly holes, especially when, as is generally the case, you
desire it to cut extra nice.

Frederick Vine, *Practical Bread-making* (1897)

Bread, like all human artefacts, is subject to fashion. And
when fashion is involved, context is everything. When young
people from affluent nations travel to the developing world
wearing ripped and ragged jeans they bring qualities of their
trousers – torn and worn – which have positive associations
within their communities, to places where these qualities have
negative associations. We tend not to associate bread with
fashion, but we should.

A few years ago I attended an international conference
in which the bread workshop opened with the moderator
throwing a loaf that had been purchased in a supermarket into
the bin. It was an industrially produced bread: soft, white, pre-
sliced and pre-packaged. To hundreds of millions of families
worldwide this was good bread. But this loaf of bread was
outside its community. To the group of people in that room
it was not just bad bread: it was not food. It was trash.

The limits of what makes a loaf bread a loaf bread are infinitely malleable. Every aspect of the loaf, its crust, crumb, colour, texture, is in the control of the baker. Even a slight change in the recipe – for example, a change in dough temperature for even a part of the leavening process – changes the finished product. Bakers create their recipes to actualize the preferences of the social group that is their primary market. What makes the study of bread such a rich field is that when all the variables are woven together into a finished loaf, that loaf means something to the people who buy it that is part of a larger narrative of their lives, of their ideas about who they are. To begin to get hold of this narrative one must step back from bread as food and look at it with the eyes of a cultural anthropologist as an object.

In loaf breads the largest part of the bread is the crumb, or inside, of the bread. A culture's idea about crumb is one of the most important ideas it can have about bread. Concepts of the ideal crumb drive every aspect of bread-making, including the choice of grain, its degree of refinement, the leavening system used and the structure of the recipe. The reason bread wheat is the largest crop in the world in terms of land used rather than a different bread grain, such as barley, is precisely because of ideas concerning the ideal crumb. The primary factors within the crumb that offer cultural markers are its inherent structure, how light it is (meaning the amount of loft it attains through rising), its texture and its colour.

Thomas Cogan wrote an influential health manual in the mid-1500s called *The Haven of Health*. It has an extensive section on bread in which Cogan describes the best by saying, 'It ought to be light, for thereby it is known that the clamminess thereof is gone.' By clamminess Cogan means stickiness. He refers to the undesirable humoral impact (the system of humours offered the leading theoretical underpinning of medicine at the time)

'Fleishmann Yeast: How to Make Bread', from *Fleishmann's Recipes* (1916).

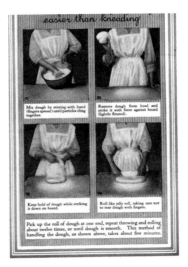

easier than kneading

Mix dough by stirring with hand (fingers spread.) until particles cling together.

Remove dough from bowl and strike it with force against board (lightly floured).

Keep hold of dough while striking it down on board.

Roll like jelly roll, taking care not to tear dough with fingers.

Pick up the roll of dough at one end, repeat throwing and rolling about twelve times, or until dough is smooth. This method of handling the dough, as shown above, takes about five minutes.

that a heavy bread could have on its consumer. Dense breads, wholegrain breads and particularly breads with rye, which was the bread grain of the poor when Cogan was writing, bake up with a crumb that is literally sticky.

A white bread leavened with yeast can double or more in size during the baking process. Owing to the nature of bran and grains other than wheat, the more bran and the more non-wheat flours included in the recipe, the less it can increase in loft. A 100 per cent wholegrain rye loaf, though technically leavened, attains very little loft through baking. By definition it does not have a 'light' crumb. In the previous chapter I postulated that a driving force behind an interest in a light crumb was that fact that it was the opposite of the crumb associated with breads of poverty.

Whatever the underlying motivation, the wide preference for a 'light' crumb drives the need for wheat flour and refined wheat flour at that. The preference for a 'light' bread drives today's milling technology to create ultra-finely milled wholegrain flour, thus allowing for much lighter wholegrain and multi-grain breads than was possible in the past. The preference for 'light' breads, even when they are brown, drives modern industrial bakers to use the latest research in the biochemistry of fermenting dough to create recipes for wholegrain wheat and multigrain breads that are soft even though it is their nature to be dense. The virtual absence of 100 per cent wholemeal rye or even wholemeal wheat bread in most artisan bakeries (those of Germany and the other countries in northern Europe's rye belt being the notable exceptions) is driven by their customers' deep aversion to 'clammy' bread and the impossibility of making a light, wholewheat bread using artisan methods. Coarse flours produce denser breads than light flours and are almost unheard of in the modern baking trade. Long before there were texts explicitly favouring the light crumb of white breads over the dense crumb of brown breads, such as that by Thomas Cogan, the interest in

Large irregular holes in the crumb of a baguette with a chewy texture, Paris, 2006.

a light crumb can be imputed by the apparently ancient association of wheat with elite breads.

A 'light' crumb can have a fine texture in which the air pockets are hard to see or an open crumb in which they are easy to see. Those air holes can be small or large, even 2 cm (nearly an inch) across. The structure can be regular or irregular. Tastes change and what was considered a well-made bread in one generation can become a poorly made or undesirable one the next, both in terms of gross crumb detail, for example, finely versus coarsely textured, and in terms of the minutiae of crumb structure, such as holes that are large and irregular or small and regular. One of the first documentable shifts in bread tastes was the shift in preference first documented in the seventeenth century from the best white bread having a fine-grained crumb produced from a heavily kneaded stiff dough, the English manchet, to the more open-crumbed bread preferred today, pain mollet, the most extreme version of

Small regular holes and crumb of baguette with soft texture, Paris, 2006.

which is probably the popular Italian ciabatta, with holes that can sometimes be described as gaping. This shift took time but can be clearly seen taking place in the seventeenth and eighteenth centuries, especially in France. If you begin to buy breads sold under the same name – such as baguettes – from different bakeries you can begin to develop a sense of today's range in crumb structure and an idea of what the details are of today's fashion by matching the qualities of the crumb to the bakery's customer base.

Finely textured, white, wheat breads tend to be soft – this is a function of how they are made – and breads with an open crumb tend to have a chewy texture. The characteristics of 'softness' and 'chewiness' can be fetishized in their own right. One driving force behind the expansion of the sourdough or *levain* bread traditions in Britain, the US and Canada is a growing consensus that a chewy crumb is 'better' and, because of differences in the way bakers tend to handle yeasted dough, sourdough breads are almost always chewier than yeasted ones.

Another aspect of crumb is colour. Since any increase in the quantity of bran and non-wheat grains makes the crumb darker in colour, there is an implicit historic association between white and light. This association, however, is no longer as clear as it was, since modern milling and baking practices, particularly those of industrial baking, have developed brown breads that have the softness of white breads. In my readings on bread going back to the mid-1500s, the brownness of brown breads never seems to have been the subject of discussion, while attributes implicit in the way country people made brown breads, notably bread density and sourness, were.

In contrast, within the purview of white breads the shade of white has long had cultural significance, as seen through explicit references to the colour ranges of white flour. Today, for example, the rejection of chemically bleached white flour by the British and American culinary elite drives artisan bakers to use flour formulated to include a distinct yellow cast, in part to differentiate their bread from the longstanding idea of a bread with a crumb as white as snow. Millers purposely produce white flours with different shades of white for specific markets. The distinctions for flours that retain bran are based largely on what percentage of bran is left in the flour and how finely it is milled.

Crumb is topped by crust. Crust is an important market for bread style. Crust can range from crisp and thick, conceptually a cracker fused onto the crumb, to thin and soft. While there is no technical reason why a thin, soft crust can't be on top of a chewy loaf with an open crumb, nor why a crisp crust can't be on top of a bread with a finely grained, soft crumb, as a matter of current custom thick and crisp tends to go with a chewy open crumb, and thin and soft with a finely textured soft crumb.

Colour is an important quality of crust. The colour of the exterior of a white wheat loaf can vary from nearly white to nearly burnt. There is a preference for nearly burnt crusts amongst a substantial population in France, and so bakeries offer loaves that are *bien cuit* (well cooked). These same breads would be unsaleable in most other countries. In the sixteenth and seventeenth centuries in much of Europe, as previously mentioned, the elite preferred a light-coloured crust on their best loaf, so bakers produced a bread that expanded in the oven like a fine baguette – except it was the colour of a par-baked loaf, such as the one depicted in Baugin's *Still-life with a Chessboard* (p. 40).

In many nineteenth-century American cookbooks the baker was advised to brush loaves fresh from the oven with water to ensure a soft crust. For centuries, in fact well into

Rye bread with a focus on crust.

the modern era, much of Europe's elite favoured a class of breads in which the crust was chipped or rasped off before service. Bread can only be chipped or rasped when hot. In an early twentieth-century recipe for a rasped roll (see p. 131) the reader was instructed to rasp off the crust and then put the rolls back in the oven. Whether this was standard practice, I do not know. But the effect was startling: a pale bread with a textured surface, and the most extraordinarily wonderful feeling when bitten into. Chipped and rasped bread was the source of the breadcrumbs that were used in so many seventeenth-century recipes. The reason for rasping was that crust was considered difficult for people who lived sedentary lives to digest, though it was believed to be fine for workers. It was also though to have other effects: the influential *Maison rustique, or, the Countrey Farme* (1616) considered crust to be 'melancholic' for these same elite diners. By the early nineteenth century the decision whether to chip or rasp was at least partly based on an aesthetic decision regarding the colour of the crust that was revealed.

Freshness is its own quality. Historically, bread was never eaten warm and, in fact, health manuals until the modern era all said that bread should not be eaten until the day after baking. Bread continues to undergo rapid chemical changes until it is cold and, as Harold McGee observes in his seminal work, *On Food and Cooking* (2004), it takes a day for bread to settle down and be in optimum condition for slicing. Rye breads tend to improve in flavour if left uncut for one to several days after baking, and many white breads are better if not sliced until the day after baking. The great French baker Lionel Poilâne of the Poilâne Bakery in Paris recommended three days for his most famous *miche*. There is thus, up to a point, an inverse relationship between freshness and taste.

Staling consists of complex reactions within the dough triggered by the migration of water from the starch granules into other parts of the bread's structure as well as the drying out of the bread by evaporation. Staling changes the way bread smells. For example, it loses its 'fresh' smell and yet, for a time, many breads develop other, pleasant tastes and aromas to replace that of 'fresh'. Rolls and breads that are designed to emphasize crisp crust – the French baguette is a classic example of this type of bread – are at their best immediately after they cool.

Staling is reversed by heating to 60°C/140°F. Reheating in the oven is effective and so is toasting. In both cases the bread should be eaten while it is still warm. Toasting combines heating with crisping and browning, the latter a process that adds its own flavours to the bread. Toast is closely identified with English bread culture and one thus tends to find the cult

Bread oven being fired, Villar d'Arène, France, 2006.

of toast more actively pursued in Britain and countries where many Britons settled, such as the USA, Canada and Australia.

Historically, household breads (as opposed to rolls and fine breads for high-status dinners) were baked once a fort-night, and sometimes much less frequently. There are country bread traditions, such as the rye loaf of the French Alps called *pain bouilli*, in which bread was only baked once a year. Among the peasantry it was standard for bread to be consumed at various stages of staling. There were different uses for breads at different points in the staling process. Breads could so stale that pieces cut or hacked out of loaves had to be soaked in water before they could be consumed. Social elites could afford to have bread baked often, or could afford to buy fresh bread from the baker, and thus staling acquired its own social markers. In my own experiments I have let breads stale to the point where they have entirely dried out and then rehydrated pieces in water. I have been amazed at how good rehydrated bread can be, particularly rye bread, and now look forward to eating rehydrated rye. A waste-not want-not approach to bread is itself an attitude of culture. In our own time the more a culture values making do and is averse to wasting food the more acceptance there is of stale and even mouldy bread. I was once served mouldy bread at a party in Lithuania and when I mentioned the mould I was met with incredulity. In the early 1990s, a time when memories of the privations of the Soviet occupation were still fresh, a little mould was not perceived as an impediment to eating the bread. That I have often been served breads in the homes of French friends that were well past their prime, including baguettes, may speak of an ancestral memory of bread as food trumping the aesthetics of freshness.

The overriding cultural interest in 'fresh' bread, particularly in the US where no degree of staling is tolerated, drives the industrial bread industry to add ingredients to their breads in order to offer customers a soft loaf that retains its softness for days, even weeks, and thus displays the cultural signs of freshness in the context of a preternatural spring.

Bread crusts are only crisp when just baked. The interest in crisp thick-crusted breads on the part of culinary elites who follow French bread fashion is undoubtedly in part a reaction against fresh-like factory breads, but it is also, in its own way, a demand for absolute freshness as crusts don't stay crisp, even for a day. Ironically, therefore, there is a way in which both a crisp crust and a soft loaf says the same thing: fresh.

The age of the grain since harvesting, type of grain, degree of refinement and flour freshness all affect the flavour of bread. Overlaying these factors are the flavours generated by the fermentation process and the way in which the baker manages the dough. In deconstructing bread flavour I think it is most helpful to focus on the range of flavours that are associated with white wheat bread. The same basic range of flavours applies to all breads but is more clearly recognized in white bread because it has an underlying neutral taste in the sense that white rice or white potatoes have neutral tastes. White bread's underlying neutral flavour can be manipulated by the baker through the fermentation process to range from neutral to slightly sweet to gradations of sour, from barely sour to very sour.

In high-status meals each dish is carefully constructed in terms of taste, colour and presentation. Bread is not the primary source of calories, but it must blend with each dish and not call attention to itself. A neutral flavour is thus usually appreciated, which may be one reason why white wheat breads have so long dominated the most formal dinner tables.

Although bread dough can be made to taste slightly sweet even without the addition of sugar, for over 100 years white yeasted loaf breads in both Britain and the USA have often included sugar, with the American breads usually including a higher percentage. Sugar was first introduced into bread in the nineteenth century by commercial bakers who used it as a dough conditioner (it softens the crumb). A taste for savoury bread with a hint of sweetness, even if subliminal, probably now underpins the addition of sugar in savoury breads. The near universal American preference in the last century for faintly sweet savoury breads is exemplified by the substitution of honey for sugar in the influential and otherwise profoundly counter-cultural *Tasahara Bread Book* (1970), to this day the bible for wholewheat breads amongst American 'hippie-style' bakers. Breads in France never include sugar, reflecting different cultural preferences and, in the British and

American context, a cultural preference now embraced along with French-style breads.

A sour flavour in bread has historically been considered an undesirable trait. Eighteenth-century French writers such as Paul-Jacques Malouin and Augustin Parmentier explicitly expressed a preference for non-sour tasting loaves. American nineteenth-century cookbooks often suggested adding an alkaline, like soda, to counteract sourness in breads that employed a sour starter. To this day, even though most breads in French artisan bakeries are made with a *levain* starter, the loaves rarely have sour tonalities, in contrast to the same style of artisan bread baked in the US and Britain. At the present time in both countries, and especially in the US, sourness is a desirable trait. To an American palate, the internationally acclaimed *pain de campagne* baked by the Poilâne bakery in Paris tastes a little flat, while to the French palate most American *levain* breads taste unacceptably sour.

Salt is such an integral part of most modern breads that it hard to step back and see salt itself as a flavour that is a parameter of taste. And yet it is. Most modern wheat breads contain a great deal of salt, typically in the range of 1.5 to 2 per cent salt by weight of flour with some bakeries using as much as 3 per cent. Although we tend not to notice, salt is one of the predominant flavours in modern bread. A check on normative cultural values can be found in the salt stipulated in bread formulations used by scientists in peer review publications, usually around 1.5 per cent.

In the period 1550–1800 in England and France recipes indicate that salt was often not used at all, or it was used so lightly that to a modern palate it would be undetectable. The first mention of a salty bread is in Randall Cotgrave's description of *pain mollet* in his 1611 French–English dictionary. *Pain mollet* is similar to the kinds of white French breads that are the most common today, breads made from dough that is soft because of a high percentage of liquid, usually water, which allows for the development of large 'eyes'. Salt plays a technical role in bread. It tightens the structure of the dough, making large eyes possible in a wet dough, thus the association between saltiness and *pain mollet* style breads. Salt also helps brown the crust. Amounts of salt in modern bread recipes, however, often go beyond what is technically required for the craft aspect of the loaf. I speculate that is in part a response to a public increasingly used to salty packaged foods.

The only area in Europe where saltless bread is still common is Tuscany. Predictably, Tuscan bread is almost uniformly reported by travellers to be 'bad'. When salt is removed from bread recipes the finished loaf tastes flat. Saltless bread is, indeed, a subtle food. Once one gets used to eating saltless bread, one begins to taste the flavour of the flour and nuances of fermentation. In my own experiments I find that breads made with freshly ground flour do not need salt. In the period I refer to when salt was missing or barely used in bread recipes flour was used immediately after grinding whereas today it is both purposely aged for at least six weeks and often not used for months or even longer. One function of salt in modern recipes may be to cover for the loss of flavour in oxidized and stale flour.

Leavening is what transforms dough into bread and it is the impact of different leavening systems, and the way the baker handles them, that determines the fundamental structures and flavours of the final product. As mentioned in chapter One, there are three primary leavening systems for bread: those based on the diffusion of steam (for thin doughs); those based on spontaneous fermentation (for sourdough loaves); and those based on the introduction of yeast by the baker. Though all three systems can be used for flatbreads, loaf

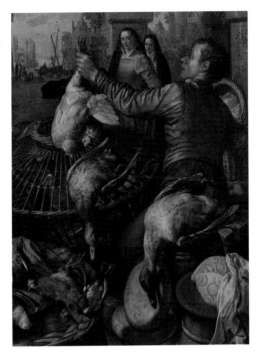

Joachim Beuckelaer, *The Four Elements: Air* (detail), 1570. Note the bread in the bottom right-hand corner.

breads can only be leavened by yeast or sourdough. Sourdough starters were and are obtained through spontaneous fermentation, often by literally just letting dough sit out at room temperature to sour. Until the later nineteenth century yeast was obtained by collecting sediment thrown off in the production of beer and using that to leaven the bread. At various times in history, one or another social group has placed value on which leavening system is used – steam alone, yeast or sourdough. Beginning in the nineteenth century chemical leavenings like baking soda (sodium bicarbonate) became widely available to bakers. Ireland is famous for its soda-leavened loaf breads, but with that notable exception, European-style loaf breads are leavened with either yeast or a sourdough starter.

Using steam alone to leaven dough limits one to flat-breads baked on a very hot surface, like a bed of embers, or in a hot oven. Examples of steam-leavened breads are the Jewish matzo and the North Indian chapatti, at least in its village form. One has to bake on a surface that is at least 400°C/752°F to create enough steam quickly enough to cause a disc of dough to rise. And rise they do. Unless pierced with many pin-pricks, as is the matzo and many flatbreads in the Caucasus, unleavened dough set to high heat often impressively blows up into round balls when baking – thus the pocket in pitta bread. However most flatbreads rely more on sourdough or yeast for leavening power or in conjunction with steam. Batter breads like crêpes or pancakes will stay gummy in their centres if they aren't leavened. Ash cakes, unless exceedingly thin, would be an indigestible lump. The lovely crispness of Scandinavian cracker-breads relies on baking a dough that is riddled with holes caused by the gases given off by the fermentation process.

Icelandic *Laufabrauð*.

Loaf breads are, by definition, a more efficient way to bake grains for a subsistence diet than are flatbreads, since one can bake a number of loaves in a single firing in a large traditional stone or clay oven. Even in large bread ovens flatbreads tend to be baked one or at most two at a time, the same as when baked slapped to the side of a tandoor oven. Since the availability of wood in most of Europe made firing large bread ovens feasible, and the climate usually allowed loaf breads to stay fresh long enough to slice for days or even weeks (or months if frozen in the winter), it is easy to understand why western Europe chose loaf breads as their staple form of bread. Steam least affects the taste of bread's primary ingredient, flour, and so is the leavening system to use if one wants to highlight the clean taste of freshly ground flour. But flatbreads have no loft; they are the opposite of 'light', and early modern health manuals stigmatized them as unhealthy. Steam leavening is a parameter of taste that European elite bread culture rejected at least 2,000 years ago.

Yeast (*Saccaramyces cerevisiae*) is a single-celled fungus that produces carbon dioxide gas as it metabolizes sugars. In bread it is the trapped gas produced by this action that produces the holes, charmingly called 'eyes' in the seventeenth century. This species of yeast does many other things as well. It produces alcohol and esters – flavours. Beer and wine yeasts can be used to make bread. Modern bread yeast varieties began to be differentiated from ale yeasts in the latter part of the nineteenth century when factories began making yeast. Today, yeast strains sold as bread yeast have been selected for gas production as, culturally in yeast breads, lightness is favoured over subtleties of flavour that might be produced by other strains of yeast.

Historically, it has long been recognized that yeast produces a lighter, softer bread, which is why elite breads such as

'Warner's Safe Yeast', an American trading card from around the late 19th century.

the eighteenth- and nineteenth-centry *pain de luxe* – for example, *pain à la Reine*, *pain de Segovie* and *pain à la Montoron* – were all yeasted.

Galen (AD 129–200/217), the Graeco-Roman writer whose ideas about health dominated the European approach to medicine and nutrition for nearly 1,400 years, favoured sourdough over yeast, asserting it was more healthful. Towards the end of the seventeenth century, the bakers of Paris obtained an injunction against bakers who were producing bread with yeast, arguing that yeast was unhealthy. They lost their legal challenge, partly on the observed fact that the English ate yeasted breads and the English were healthy. Elite breads notwithstanding, most eminent French bread writers in the eighteenth century wrote unfavourably of yeast, including Malouin and Parmentier. *Levain* breads remain the dominant style of leavened bread in French bakeries. Along with the adoption of *levain* breads among a large number of Anglophone artisan bakeries has also come a distrust of yeast. A sourdough loaf in a grocery store near me proudly declares on its package: 'All natural and baker's yeast free.'

Sourdough is literally sour dough. A flour and water dough left at room temperature will begin to rise of its own accord. Flour and water mixed into a batter and left out at room temperature will also sour and begin to bubble within a few days. The batter or left-out dough is colonized by bacteria and yeast in the ratio of approximately 100:1. The bacteria and the varieties of yeast that colonize the dough work in a symbiotic relationship to digest the sugars, producing carbon dioxide in the process – the gas, as with yeasted breads, that is trapped in the structure of the dough and makes loaf breads possible. The sourdough process can be managed to create a bread with a neutral taste, a sweet taste – particularly when using rye flour – or a sour taste.

Historically, in the British context, sourdough breads were always associated with poverty, since anyone with means could

Pan Picado/Andaluz, Madrid.

make their bread with yeast, either because they brewed their own ale or because they could afford to buy yeast from the brewer, thus ensuring the lightest, sweetest-tasting loaf. In the French context, in which brewing was less common, using sourdough as a leavening was usually a necessity. Even so, a sour-tasting sourdough implied poverty and provincial taste. Through published French recipes it is possible to see that in elite households, as in French bakeries today, *levain* dough tended to be managed so the bread would not taste sour. Since yeast dough can be managed to produce a bread that is virtually indistinguishable from a *levain* bread managed by the baker not to be sour, certainly in the modern context in which yeast is always easily available, the preference for one leavening system over another is itself largely a matter of fashion.

Bread is such a complex product that there is virtually no limit to aspects of bread that determine people's preferences, both intrinsic and extrinsic to the recipe. Concepts such as 'natural' or 'traditional' become associated with positive cultural values and breads that are not 'natural' or 'traditional' are then burdened with negative values. Few of us willingly eat mouldy bread but calcium propionate, a salt that retards fungal growth, is only found in industrial breads. If the cultural value of human ingenuity was given more weight among the culinary elites than the concept of a 'natural' bread, then artisan-style breads could begin expanding their ingredient list to include, for example, preservatives. Certain buyers look for flour used in the bread to be 'organic' even though the taste and nutritional qualities of breads made to the same recipe with equivalent organic and non-organic flour are for all practical purposes the same. And the list goes on as the complexity of bread's manufacture enmeshes it in so many aspects of culture. Good, bad and indifferent are judgements of loaves that are inevitably rooted in time, place and social class. Bread is an interesting story because this is so. It is always a pleasure to join the fray and critique the bread on the table, but once we start stepping back to look at the loaves with the eye of a historian the qualities that underpin the judgements of good, bad and indifferent look increasingly arbitrarily assigned. The only qualities that are true for all time in all places are issues of craft as defined by local custom. If a given bread is deemed best with certain characteristics then, certainly, as a matter of craft, it must have them. If the crust must be deeply coloured, and it is not, then it is a poor loaf. Whatever the indicators of taste for one's time and group, the best loaf will meet them.

4
World of Bread: An Eccentric Travelogue

Foods travel. They always have. While it may seem they travel faster than they did in the past, the underlying substance of the travelling remains unchanged – they travel in the context of cuisines and changing world-views. The widespread international adoption of the baguette, and more recently the Italian ciabatta, is part of a package of ideas, the most obvious being that in the context of dinner a touch of the foreign is a good thing.

There is nothing like naked colonialism to change world-views quickly – and local bread cultures along with it. The world-striding European colonial powers of Spain, France and Britain spread their breads to their colonies. Thus Mexico and South America are awash with wheat breads, many with direct ties back to the Iberian Peninsula; *petit pain* is hawked on the streets of Cambodia; and loaf breads made of wheat flour baked in tins are sold in bakeries throughout the British Commonwealth. The world-striding military and economic power of the neo-colonial US offers the paradigmatic modern example of the swift global spread of a leavened bread in the form of America's hamburger bun, a bread that has spread throughout the world in the figurative blink of an eye. The current spread of European-style leavened breads to Asia is part of the changes in diet and taste that seem to be driven by peacefully established trade routes and the ease of modern mass communication. While there is a level of international homogeneity in the world of loaf bread, especially in the internationally recognized named breads, like baguette, and in the ubiquitous factory sandwich bread, even these breads tend to change as they cross cultural borders. The Cambodian *petit pain* has no salt, which keeps it crisper for longer in a humid climate; in North America the British sandwich loaf that is otherwise identical tends to be made with a little more sugar than in Britain, though the taste is still subliminal; and in Asia, where loaf breads are a comparatively recent introduction, brown breads are only beginning to make an appearance, and loaf breads tend to be both ultra-white and overtly sweet. Bread culture can vary significantly from country to country and, though it is outside the scope of this survey, bread culture may vary within countries, too.

In this brief overview I introduce six loaf bread cultures: those of France, Mexico, Germany, Russia, Britain and the US.

Grocery display of industrial breads, Nairobi, Kenya.

In all cases, in these countries, and in almost any other country one chooses, there are always two distinct systems of commercial bread manufacture and distribution – industrial-scale breads distributed through grocery stores, and artisan-produced breads distributed at least in part through neighbourhood bakeries that often also include on-site baking. There is also increasingly a third baking system that mediates between the two, which is the baking-off of partially baked loaves in bakeries situated within grocery stores. Some countries, in this sample notably Britain and America, have vibrant home-baking traditions. As this is a travelogue its focus is on breads you might encounter as a tourist. I close this chapter with flatbreads to offer at least a hint of what to expect when one leaves cultures whose breads are primarily influenced by European culture.

Generally, in each of the loaf-bread countries mentioned in this chapter, the industrially produced breads tend to be the cheapest and also the more utilitarian, with pre-sliced sandwich breads being the most common type of industrial bread. These breads tend to be more alike country-to-country than bakery breads, but this said, industrial breads are not homogeneous and there are differences both between countries and within countries in the industrial breads baked for different social groups. But it is through artisan bakers that countries express their bread ideals even if, in practice, the industrial bread sector dwarfs that of artisan bakers. The subject of this chapter is artisan bread – breads created by what our industrial society deems to be small-scale production processes. In the modern context this actually means baking with the use of machines, particularly mixers, but loaves are often formed by hand and the production line isn't integrated.

I begin with France because France has long exerted an influence on cuisines outside its national border. The French baguette is known throughout the world. The French tend

Quotidian Bakery, New York City.

to have confidence in themselves and in the overriding excellence of their culinary traditions. Setting aside all questions regarding France's breads' comparative qualities with other national bread traditions, what clearly stands out is the long-standing French confidence in its own bread tradition as being both good and complete. As you walk around the non-immigrant parts of French cities it is notable that foreign-style breads are rarely encountered in artisan bakeries. Where is the ciabatta that one finds in Madrid, the German rye one finds in London, the foreign bread equivalent to the baguette or *pain de campagne* one finds in New York? France exports bread ideas and, with the notable exception of industrial pre-packaged breads sold in grocery stores, it tends not to import them.

Nicolas de Bonnefons first articulated French confidence in their own bread in 1651. In the introduction to the bread recipes in his book *Les Delices de la Campagne* he says 'people of all nations . . . are in accord; in Paris one eats the best bread in all the world'. French public opinion has not changed and many an international traveller would still agree with Bonnefons' characterization. One central aspect of French bread culture, and one reason that it exerts such an intellectual force internationally, is that the recipes are created with an unusually consistent set of structured concepts. As long ago as the mid-seventeenth century Bonnefons' bread recipes demonstrated a disciplined methodology for bread-making that implied conscious control of the dough to obtain precise tastes and textures. This was not found in bread recipes of the time from other nations and, indeed, is still rarely found outside the French bread tradition. Bonnefons reinforced the implicit relationship between recipe and taste by suggesting breaking off a small piece of dough and baking it to check the flavour so one could make adjustments before baking the batch. There is something deep in the French cultural attitude towards bread, a striving towards an explicitly conceived concept of bread excellence, that makes it more self-aware than most other bread cultures.

Floating flour mill on the Seine, Paris, anonymous 18th-century print.

A version of fougasse, Tours, France, 2003.

France, of course, is not immune to the forces of modern economics. And any time the greatness of one's product is considered axiomatic the stage is set for living the parable of the emperor who has no clothes: in this case, breads that look spectacular but don't taste it. As France has explicitly set itself such a high standard for so long it seems fair to ask as one tastes one's way around French bakeries – is this loaf well made, is this loaf worth writing home about and, if so, why?

What will you find on a tour of central Parisian bakeries? I specify central Paris because France is a modern country with a substantial immigrant population that has brought its own bread traditions to France. As of this writing, these traditions are fairly separate from each another. One does not find Algerian semolina breads in central Parisian bakeries. Perhaps one day a sign of deeper cultural integration between old and new France will be a blending of breads from immigrant traditions into the national mainstream.

Parisian bakery with unusual breads.

The modern mainstream French baking tradition is based on the cult of wheat. It is a tradition that, more than other European bread traditions, celebrates crust. Look at any central Parisian bread display. Crust! The breads are rarely baked in tins. Instead, they are formed in baskets and between the folds of folded cloth, then baked directly on the floor of the oven. Top crust is maximized. Bread displays celebrate shades of brown from golden to near black, with some breads literally being on the edge of burnt. The slash marks that scar the crusts and allow breads to expand in the oven seem also to be part of the French bread culture's affection for shades of brown and the extemporaneous patterns of the expansion scars.

In general, the French baking trade embraces sourdough starters – *levain* – as the leavening of choice. Sourdough starters need time, and time is money, and thus the pressures of the modern world push bakers to cut their tradition's corners. As you decide which bakeries to sample breads from, choose those that announce in the bakery window that their bread is *pain à l'ancienne*. This designation does not mean the bread is made as it was made in the eighteenth century but it does mean that their baking methods meet at least the minimum standards of the government regulation that seeks to establish a floor on bread quality as currently conceived. It is always easy to travel and pick a fight, but I think it best to travel and sample what a country puts forward as its best product.

French bakeries display a substantial array of differently named breads but, as befits a country with a classic cuisine, the same dough baked into different shapes produces breads with different names. A bakery with a dozen breads might only actually be making three different types of dough. For example, the dough used for the baguette is also used for the *petit pain* and the *ficelle*. Buy one of each to get a sense of how changing shape can change the very sense of the dough.

Mexico! Mexican bakeries are like no other. Instead of standing in front of a counter to be served, which is a standard international custom, Mexican bakeries are self-service. One

One of many kinds of imaginatively shaped roll found in Mexican bakeries.

Bread ovens in Guanjuato, Mexico.

walks into the display area. In bakeries of any size one is usually surrounded on three sides by a multi-tiered array of breads often from waist-height to eye-level. One walks around the bakery holding an aluminum tray and a pair of stainless steel tongs to select what one wants. As the tray and tongs implies, the Mexican bakery specializes in small breads, rolls that fall into two broad categories – sweet yeasted rolls – *pan dulce* – and savoury rolls like the crusty white *bolillo*. Artisan loaf breads tend to be sold in covered markets.

Standing in the middle of a Mexican bakery scanning the baskets filled with multifariously shaped and coloured breads one stands within an Ali Baba's cave of doughy jewels. There are the distinctive *concha*, breads with sugar crusts dyed pink, red and white. Some are stamped with elaborate steel cutters that overlay complex patterns into crusts that would be complexly patterned even without them. Both savoury and sweet, there are rolls in a multitude of shapes. The Mexican bakery reveals a creative baking culture that is a potential source of fresh inspiration to the world's artisan bakers, whose focus tends to be more on modern European practice.

Knotted rolls provide an example of design exuberance that is easily adaptable to many standard bread doughs. Over a period of several days I purchased 22 unenriched crusty yeasted rolls at a bakery in Guanajuato, each baked into a different shape. The dough had been rolled into a thin snake and then cut and twisted to form braids and knots.

Mexican bakers have preserved, more or less intact, a few European bread traditions that are no longer common in Europe. For example, there are seventeenth-century Dutch still-lifes that depict sliced breads spread with butter and sprinkled with sugar. This delicacy is sold in every Mexican bakery under the name *mantecato*. Most bakeries sell rolls that have had the crumb removed and been rebaked sprinkled with

Milk bread for sale in Mexico City.

A bakery in Shanghai, China, in 2010.

sugar. There is a documented French practice from the six-teenth century of removing the crumb, sprinkling the bread with alcohol and anise and rebaking it. One finds in Mexican bakeries a blending of the European with the Mexican, and in particular with the playful part of Mexican culture.

Lest I leave you with a dream of Mexican bakeries that un-realistically implies that the Mexican baking trade as a whole is composed of small bakeries producing an astonishing array of interesting baked goods through the exploitation of inex-pensive labour, I should mention that the Mexican industrial baking giant, Bimbo, is one of the largest food companies in the world and well on its way to achieving its goal of being the world's largest industrial baking enterprise. It has huge holdings outside Mexico, including in the US, and is an agent for advancing loaf bread culture in China.

Borders often make for interesting studies. Cross from France into Germany to find a radically different bread culture.

The German loaf bread tradition embraces variety in ways the French does not. There is also a north/south divide: for example, there are more aromatic seeded breads and more wheat breads in the south and more pure rye breads in the north. Taken as a group German bakeries offer a richness and depth of loaf bread styles that is unparalleled in other countries. One finds the whitest of white breads and the darkest of dark breads. There are tinned loaves and loaves that were baked outside tins in rounds or ovals after having been shaped in baskets. Alone among the major European bread traditions, the German embraces the breads of European poverty – dense, deeply flavoured rye breads, true wholewheat loaves like *Vollkornbrot* and dense wheat/rye maslin combinations such as the *Roggenmischbrot*. The German tradition also features an elaborate modern fantasy of seeded breads that makes visiting German bakeries a visual delight. Often breads are clothed with seeds: sunflower, flax, sesame, poppy. Seeds are also often incorporated into breads, in many cases making dense breads denser, as in some modern versions of the slow-baked rye meal pumpernickel. Caraway, fennel, coriander and aniseed also often flavour breads, especially in the south. German seeded breads remind us of the countryside's fertility, the glowing golden of fields of wheat, the sky-blue of flax.

You will also often find loaves decorated simply with a dusting of white wheat flour prior to baking. This accentuates the topographical richness of loaves that split open when baking, highlighting the organic patterns created by the expansion of the loaf in the oven to create richly textured natural decoration.

A source of German bread dynamism is clearly in its celebration of its own home-grown bread traditions. Much of Germany is better suited to growing rye than wheat – and this was especially true in the past before synthetic fertilizers.

In contrast with France, however, which rejected their own longstanding rye tradition, twentieth-century Germany embraced it as part of several distinct philosophical traditions that found inspiration in country life.

Interest in country life and country traditions is a longstanding German intellectual project – the Brothers Grimm who so famously collected folktales in the nineteenth century, were part of that project. The specific bread tradition we see in bakeries today was heavily influenced by the nineteenth and early twentieth-century *Lebensreform Bewegung* (Life Reform Movement) that, among other things, celebrated wholegrain breads as a source of healthiness in contrast to the refined wheat breads of urban industrialization. Ideas of the *Lebensreform* remained influential throughout the twentieth century, including the Nazi movement and in the later twentieth-century reaction against industrial farming, industrial bread and modern life in general. The Germans eat more bread per capita than any other people in Europe and it is likely that there is a correlation between consumption patterns and the combination of apparent healthiness with deep flavour that is a hallmark of so much German bread. More clearly than in most other countries German artisan bakeries illustrate the power of an idea – and as it is an idea that creates breads that are very specifically German they make a fascinating study of the links between bread and culture.

Russia. When I did an online search for Moscow bakeries, one of the first listings was for Le Pain Quotidien, an international chain of French bakeries. On the same day I found Le Pain Quotidien there was an article in a British newspaper, the *Guardian*, reporting that a few days earlier the Russian prime minister and president had breakfasted together on milk and brown bread. This was to show their ties to the humble folk in the countryside.

Dense, dark loaves made with 100 per cent rye flour, black breads are associated with Russia. Though Russia is at the centre of the Northern European rye belt, and Russians do eat rye, in 2003 per capita consumption of rye bread in Poland was 35 kg (77 lb) while it was only 8 kg (18 lb) in Russia, less than Germany and the countries of Scandinavia. In Russia bread in general and rye in particular is stigmatized as a cheap food. As of this writing, bread produced in Russia is sold under price controls. In contrast, you will find that in Moscow and St Petersburg imported breads can cost as much as a bottle of wine. While only two decades ago, during the Soviet period, the typical bakery effectively sold only one kind of bread – dense and brown – today big city bakeries sell dozens of types of breads, reflecting many bread traditions from a wide range of countries. Russia is still a country in transition and is working out its cultural identity. As a visitor to Russia you will find in its bakeries reflections of change and politics. While Germans are rightly proud of their country bread traditions, it is no longer a pride that is linked to government-promoted concepts of national identity. Today in Russia your decision as to what bread you put on your table, in addition to all the other messages that breads might give that have been discussed in previous chapters, may also say something about your ideas about Russia's place in the world.

An examination of bread in the UK provides a powerful illustration of evolution in culinary traditions. This is a period of profound change in Britain's foodways, and that change is reflected in significant changes in bread culture, most notably an embrace of the sourdough baking traditions of France, Germany and of today's American artisan bread movement. It is a remarkable time to wander through British bakeries. Bread traditions that had been stable for centuries have been upended with remarkable suddenness.

It is hard to overestimate the historic significance of the widespread adoption of sourdough breads by today's bakers in the UK. For centuries, if not millennia, British bakers favoured yeast over sourdough leavening systems. But increasingly there are British bakeries specializing in breads from the sourdough traditions of France (*levain*), America (San Francisco sourdough) and Germany (sour rye). Even when bakeries don't specialize in sourdough breads at least a few sourdough breads are being integrated into what is becoming a standard bakery mix of yeasted and sour-leavened breads. Another way to think about it is that for almost 500 years British culinary culture, despite the closest possible ties with France, rejected its *levain* tradition, keeping to its yeast-leavened loaves even while its aristocracy and upper classes often openly admired and adopted French food for their formal table.

In the twentieth century the introduction and widespread acceptance of industrial bread was emblematic of revolutionary changes that were taking place at all levels of British society and culture. The changes in bread culture taking place now are no less significant and point to equally momentous cultural shifts. In addition to an openness to the sourdough tradition, other foreign breads, in particular the Italian ciabatta, are now staples of the bakery shelf. As always, there is a tension between being open to new foods and losing the old ones. At big city markets, such as those in London and Edinburgh, what had been traditional British yeast-leavened loaves such as the cottage, coburg, bloomer, farmhouse and tin are virtually nonexistent, as are the many small breads that were the staple of the breakfast table and the afternoon tea. Instead market bakers tend to make sourdough loaf breads. Contrast this rejection of British bread traditions with the celebration of the traditional products of British butchers and fishmongers.

To get a sense of the evolving bread scene, whether one is from Britain or visiting from abroad, I'd pay particular attention to bakeries in city centres, in affluent suburbs, the bread sections of speciality grocery stores and market stall bakers. One of the most popular stalls in the Edinburgh Castle Terrace market is a German baker with a sourdough rye.

Of course, as someone from abroad, it is the British breads that interest me the most. I personally love the soft white tinned loaf that was for so long the featured bakery bread. It is a yeasted bread that was long made with some milk, a little sugar and a little fat (see pp. 130–31 for a recipe.) It is delicious with British standbys – cheese and chutney or butter and Marmite. You will tend to find tinned breads and at least one traditional English loaf in village bakeries, bakeries in tourist towns, like Rye, and in the baking sections of grocery stores catering to a more mass market.

The British, of course, love their toast, with toast being a major use of bread in Britain. Toasting reverses staling, so whether the bread is fresh or stale, once toasted and served hot it is crisp on the outside and soft in the middle. Nineteenth-century British literature is full of references to toasting bread on the end of a fork in front of a coal fire. The toasting-fork gave way in the early decades of the twentieth century to the convenience of the electric toaster, which was invented at the end of the nineteenth century; toast became more prosaic in the process. Toast is a classic example of bread use that demonstrates the relationship between use and bread style. The ciabatta, baguette and big-holed sour French breads don't lend themselves to the English style of toast, which is spread with butter and often also with jam while still hot. If one sees that artisan bakeries don't offer breads that lend themselves to English-style toasting one can probably infer that many shoppers are supplementing the new-style breads with a more traditional loaf bread purchased elsewhere or with a packaged, pre-sliced industrial bread purchased in a grocery store.

The US is a continent-sized country of 300 million people, 33 million of whom were born in other countries, with a bread tradition closely allied with that of Britain. Industrial bread dominates the American bread trade as it does in so many other countries but artisan bread is well integrated into changing American foodways. Artisan bakers exist in every city and neighbourhood bakeries are undergoing a revival.

There are many American cities with extensive districts where virtually all commerce is conducted in a language other than English, for example, Korean, Spanish or Russian. While the country is clearly tied together by a unified culture and mass market retail brings similar stores to every region, regionalism, from fine-scaled regionalism based on neighbourhood culture to broader scale regionalism based on larger-scale historic factors, does mean that if you search you will find a deep and varied array of breads with their related bread traditions that stand outside mainstream American bread cultures. Also, because the population is so large, even a culturally minor subculture might involve tens of thousands or even millions of people and, in reference to bread, an entire world of bakeries and bread customs. For the adventurous, search out ethnic communities in any American city you visit. The Mexican bakeries are not as elaborate as those found in Mexico, but they are Mexican and you can find lovely *pan dulce* to take back to your home or hotel room to eat with milk, coffee or hot chocolate. If you find that there is a large Lithuanian, Russian or Polish community somewhere – go there. You may find pure rye breads being sold, and in the oddities of immigration and cultural memory it could easily be that these breads are more 'authentically' Lithuanian, Russian or Polish

Neighbourhood artisan bakery, northern California.

than breads in the home countries, as recipes often reflect the time when the immigrants arrived and may not reflect changes in bread culture back home. For example, rye breads in Lithuania are increasingly being sweetened with honey, which they never were in the past, while the American Lithuanian recipe is still likely to be made with nothing more than rye flour, water and salt.

As in Britain, for most of the twentieth century wheat breads baked in tins were the mainstay of the mainstream bakery shelf. These usually included some sugar and fat in keeping with by then accepted custom. While Britain retained a tradition of 'brown breads', by the 1960s American wheat breads were almost always white. Then suddenly everything began to change. Tectonic cultural forces began fracturing the country, initiating cultural processes that are still at play. In rejecting the lives of their parents the young people who protested against the Vietnam War and identified themselves with the hippie movement also rejected their food, including their bread. This rejection came primarily through the rejection of white flour. While now few and far between, there remain bakeries inspired by this first reappraisal of American bread. They tend to be found in college towns, such as Ithaca, New York, and in small towns where there is still a concentration of people who embrace the hippie ideals, like Big Sur, California. Hippie bakeries, even updated versions of them, are a treasure to find as they offer a range and style of whole-wheat breads that are becoming increasingly rare but that clearly demonstrate how sub-cultures can invent breads and bread traditions to reflect and proclaim counter-cultural values.

The hippies were not the only Americans in the 1960s who were rejecting the food of their parents. Many of their parents were rejecting that food, too, only differently. This other food revolution can, in shorthand, be attributed to Julia Child who said, in effect, turn your back on canned and packaged foods of the 1950s, come into the kitchen and cook for taste, for flavour and for the joy of eating. I think cultural historians will show how the hippie movement and the movement that the publication of *Mastering the Art of French Cooking*, written by Child, Simone Beck and Louisette Bertholle in 1961, galvanized came together into the food revolution that continues today. The most influential bread recipe Julia Child published was a recipe for baguettes. No sugar in the dough; no oil; a crisp crackling crust and, of course, it isn't baked in a tin.

American bakeries are now full of French breads. Francophile bakeries tend to dominate in large cities and in affluent communities. Even their interior designs often reference French bakeries. Beginning in the last decades of the twentieth century American bakers, allied with an evolving new American cuisine based on organic food and an amalgam of southern

French and Italian culinary traditions, created a new American bread tradition. It combined the sour taste of the indigenous San Francisco sourdough bread tradition with the French *levain* tradition, which offered a sophisticated body of work to study. In many parts of the country sour-tasting French *levain* bread is the dominant style of bread in artisan bakeries, as well as the taste profile of the most elite breads. *Levain* breads pushed out what had been traditional American yeasted breads. Even more than in Britain it can be hard to find a basic white yeasted sandwich loaf apart from pre-sliced pre-packaged industrial bread on the grocery store shelf.

Since sourness is the most salient hallmark of what makes American French breads American, I'd seek out *pain de campagne* in different bakeries and taste for qualities of sour. As sour is a sought-after feature the baker is likely to be proud of the taste and will be happy to explain to you how it was achieved. Artisan bakeries usually produce baguettes and the internationally famed Italian ciabatta. More uniquely American, in many parts of the country bakeries offer the Ashkenazim Jewish challah, a lightly enriched braided yeast bread. Two less common breads associated with the Jewish immigration of the early twentieth century that are worth tracking down are 'Jewish rye' and the American version of pumpernickel. Neither of these breads contain much rye and both offer rich examples of how recipes may radically change when crossing borders.

Borders are everywhere, although they are not always obvious. Bread can help you see them. There are borders within every big city and between every city and the countryside that surrounds it. Borders both metaphysical and physical may separate flatbreads from loaf breads. The Orthodox Church and the Catholic Church differ as to whether Jesus ate leavened bread or flatbread on the night of his last supper. There are borders that separate the cultures of loaf breads from those of flatbreads that mark lines of violent conflict. Thus some borders of religion, nationality and tribe could be seen as being demarcated, in part, by the loft of their breads.

The flatbread tradition is massively complex and is little documented in the bread literature of the loaf bread countries.

As a traveller or tourist you will find that the vast regions dominated by flatbreads, including north Africa, the near East, the Caucasus, Central Asia and northern India, are areas where firewood is often scarce and where the climate is often hot and dry. These are poor conditions for loaf breads and, indeed, loaf breads are rare or even nonexistent. In these regions industrialization has not reached the levels it has in most of the loaf-bread countries. While you will find breads in modern supermarkets produced by industrial-scale bakeries, more often you will find breads produced by small-scale bakeries and in small villages in people's homes. In many big cities, like New Delhi, you will see small production bakeries set up on the side of the road, here for the pitta-like chapatti and roti, and for other breads in other parts of the flatbread world. Most of the breads you encounter in the flatbread regions are made from wheat, although if you are attentive you will find breads made with other flours as well, such as barley. Arid countries, like Egypt, where bread still accounts for a large percentage of the daily caloric intake, don't have the water to grow sufficient wheat for local consumption so they import much of their grain. This said, search out breads made with local flours whenever you are in the countryside.

Because many parts of the flatbread regions are still very poor you may find that ancient social systems surrounding grain growing, milling and baking are still intact. Exploring these systems along with the use of bread in the local cuisine is likely to prove a more insightful exploration of the local

Pain de campagne, with an imaginative pattern baked into the crust.
Balthazar Bakery, New York City.

culture than a mere cataloguing of local breads. For example, there are areas in India where you will still find subsistence grain agriculture in which families produce their daily bread through every step of the process from growing through milling to baking. Watching and even helping a woman mill flour for the family's bread on a rotary quern will offer you the kinds of insights into culture, life and bread that are not found in books.

Flatbreads are made on any number of baking systems and as bakeries tend to be plentiful in flatbread countries, one of the pleasures of travelling for flatbread is visiting bakeries. This is usually a very social activity and especially so for a tourist. In many countries one can expect to collect a small group, or even a crowd of dozens of people, watching you watch the baking, so never be in a hurry. Sometimes you will see domed bread ovens, like those used in Europe, but throughout the Caucasus and into Central Asia and India the tandoor oven familiar from Indian restaurants is more common. In a tandoor the fire sits at the bottom of a ceramic-lined pit. The top of the pit, which is the oven, is open and the baker often sits beside the oven opening where he or she can lean into the opening to slap bread onto the side of the oven where it sticks and bakes. Baking times are short. The long thin *lavash* of Armenia is made this way as may be the smaller round chapatti of India. In many countries it is common to see street bakeries in which bread is stretched over what looks like the bottom of a large wok. These griddles are often fired by gas.

No flatbreads are entirely flat. You will encounter breads that are a few centimetres thick, often griddle baked. These are typically the thickness of an English muffin, though, like the Algerian *khobz eddar*, in its modern form a yeast-leavened bread often made with semolina, it can be the diameter of a dinner plate. Both these thicker flat breads and the thinner styles are sometimes pricked with needles to make tiny holes in the dough before baking. This prevents them puffing up during baking. The patterns made by the pricks can be beautiful. If you are lucky and can get into the countryside in regions where nomadic traditions survive, or people are exceedingly poor, you may find breads like the chapatti or oval bubbly Kazakh *taba-nan* baked in embers.

Of course, everywhere, the breads serve cuisine. You cannot really appreciate a flatbread in Kazakhstan, a *pane dolce* in Mexico, a brown bread in Germany, a sandwich bread in America, a baguette in France without eating it with people the way they eat it. So remember, wherever you are, be friendly, ask lots of questions and if you are invited to a meal, say yes.

5
Bread in the Twenty-first Century

The relationship described in the Book of Genesis between bread and its producer was one in which the required hard labour of planting, harvesting, winnowing and milling was so horrific and life-numbing that the bread was the literal embodiment of the awful consequences of the expulsion from Eden. For most people, from the invention of agriculture at least ten thousand years ago until recent times, bread meant being trapped in a Sisyphus-like embrace of endless sweaty toil. As industrialization took hold in Europe and North America agricultural practices became more efficient and ever fewer of us worked the land, milled grain or baked bread. One can say that as industrialization progressed both individually and collectively we grew ever further removed from grain agriculture, grain processing and the necessity of baking our daily loaf.

In Europe the final break with the ancient relationship between the bread on one's table and the family's agricultural and domestic work took place in the years just after the end of the Second World War through forced collectivization in the lands controlled by the Soviet Union and advancing affluence in the rest of Europe. In the US and Canada the collapse of this ancient relationship had occurred decades earlier.

This is the first century since the invention of agriculture in which it can be said that loaf breads no longer have a foundation within the life of the North American or European countryside. While country breads may never have had much relation with breads of the court and the 'upstairs' table of wealthy households, the demise of these ancient relationships between growing, milling, baking and eating is yet another indication that in many ways we as humans have entered a new phase in our cultural lives, one profoundly different from that of our ancestors. It is no coincidence that the popular French *pain de campagne* is a bread that was popularized after the Second World War, after there was effectively no authentic bread of the countryside. While the bread itself is not new – there are clear references to this type of bread in the eighteenth-century writings of Antoine-Augustin Parmentier – it is a comparatively refined bread and its association with the countryside is more a modern conceit than an ethnographic reality. Breads of the deep country were substantially

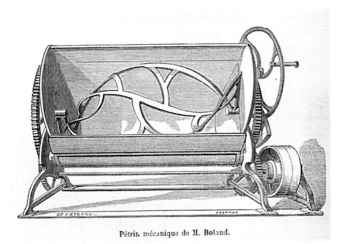

Pétrin mécanique de M. Boland.

French mechanical kneader, late 19th century .

French bakery, mid-19th century.

denser. Considering that that there have been so many breaks in ancient traditions within loaf breads' cultural centre in Europe and North America, and so recently, it is not surprising that those closest to these traditions, in particular the contemporary craft baker, look backwards for inspiration. But as we cannot manufacture bread in the same way it was manufactured in the past – the back-injuring physical labour involved in working large batches of dough is inconsistent with modern ethics – it is not precisely accurate to describe the modern craft baker as backwards-looking in the narrowest meaning of the term. Taken as a group, the intellectual work of craft bakers is devoted to developing and perfecting new bread making systems that replicate values that were present in historic loaves but employ modern equipment at key points in the production system. *Pain de campagne* is of a piece with the emergence of farmers' markets, heirloom vegetables, farmhouse cheeses and so much more that is being embraced as good and important in both Britain and America that derives inspiration from the culture of a rural past.

Another significant break in longstanding traditions surrounding loaf breads is the baking of breads at home, which used to be done out of necessity. Until fairly recently, in villages and cities, many families baked bread because it was the most economically viable option. Today bread is baked at home for reasons of necessity only in pockets of extreme rural poverty, for example, among the Gypsies of Romania. Otherwise, for all practical purposes, home bread-making is now recreational.

I divide contemporary baking into three discrete traditions: recreational home baking, commercial craft baking and industrial baking. While the breads produced by these three traditions have many shared preferences – a preference for wheat being an obvious one – they tend to produce breads that are different from each other even if an increasing number of home bakers' breads replicate those of the craft bakery.

Roma bread oven, Deva, Romania, *c.* 2004.

The twentieth century was one in which many culinary choices contracted. It was the century of the mass market. Despite the plethora of apparent choices in the shops there is a sense in which the twentieth century ended up being the one-size-fits-all century. Looking ahead from the very beginning of the twenty-first century it seems that there are now structural forces at work that are bringing back diversity to areas where it had seemed lost forever. In many areas, including the culinary, the mass market is breaking up into a multitude of speciality markets, some of which may still be large but others are very small. While the import of these changes may be exaggerated it does seem even as the centrifugal forces seem ascendant centripetal forces are gaining ground.

The Internet and associated developments are driving the growth of centripetal forces. Still new and rapidly evolving communication systems make it possible to bring together people who have similar interests but who are separated geographically. We are still so much at the beginning of this revolutionary change that it is hard to see all its consequences. One unanticipated consequence is that farmers are beginning to grow varieties of bread grains that had long been out of commercial production because even a tiny crop can be successfully marketed to small but focused markets. This is potentially significant to the way in which breads will change during this century because flour matters – different types of wheat can have very different baking characteristics, producing very different breads from the same recipe.

The Internet tends to spread ideas as well as best practice. While it is yet unclear where this will take bread in this century, the fact that so many books are now available online, with more added daily, means that many old ideas, in this case breads that have long been out of favour, or that were known only to a small region, can be found by virtually anyone and given a new life in a new context. The plethora of online videos – and the emergence of the new hybrid book/video – means that one can study and re-study the physical technique of making breads from a range of cultural traditions in a way that had been impossible before. By century's end it is easy to imagine that all historic bread texts will have been aggregated, and that videos will have become more professional as well as systematized. While many ancient ways have just ended, new ways are being created. Bread culture tends to develop fairly slowly and yet there has been a significant shift in bread styles over the previous 40 years. The next shift in bread styles is likely to be even more dynamic as so many complex new forces are at work.

With the ending of rural traditions the home baker is effectively the only amateur baker left. The home baker thus fills the niche that country bakers used to fill. Historically, as with so much else around the house, bread baking was a female art. As industrialization progressed, and as bread left the home, the transmission of bread recipes shifted from oral instructions given by a mother to her daughter to written instructions offered by one stranger to another. While bread-making has not become masculinized to the extent of the management of live fire within the home (men tend to be the ones who light the fireplace fire, the barbecue fire and the campfire), in a radical departure from past practice domestic bread baking is now often done by men, even as cakes and pastries remain the purview of women. As male and female culture differs, recreational bread baking has already changed in response to the change in sex of the baker. There is a distinct male domestic baking sub-culture that is focused on the perfection of technique in emulation of craft bakers in contrast to the more recent use of urban home-baked bread to express the woman's role as the one who nurtures the family. For example, in the

An American recipe pamphlet published as an advertisement for 'Sloan's Headache Wafers', *c.* 1905.

US, the overwhelming majority of bakers who participate in the Bread Bakers Guild of America's Internet discussion group and identify themselves as a 'SHB' (Serious Home Baker) are men.

Published bread recipes have long been influenced by the commercial practices of their times. This was true of the first published English bread recipes by William Harrison in the 1500s and continues to this day. To give two specific examples, the introduction of sugar into British and American home bread recipes in the later nineteenth century reflected changes in the baking trade, as did the introduction into the home kitchen of the electric mixer in the twentieth century, a tool that is clearly not necessary for one or two loaves of bread. In baking books today one is beginning to see the introduction of malt into home bread recipes, increasing use of technical talk about such matters as the role of enzymes in dough fermentation, the introduction of the 'autolyse' resting period (where the water and flour is mixed without salt and leavening and then left to rest, usually for twenty minutes before the rest of the ingredients are added), as well as the use of 'baker's math' reflecting the influence of today's most advanced artisan bakers. The bread machine, beloved of millions of home bakers, is a miniature in-line bread factory in which the mixing, kneading, forming, proving and baking all take place in a single machine without the intervention of the human hand. It is a contribution to the home baker from the industrial rather than the artisanal baking tradition and thus represents industrial ideas rejected by most artisan bakers – and yet these table-top factories are beloved of millions of home bakers and can produce excellent loaves of bread. These machines could be made significantly more sophisticated with the addition of refrigeration coils, sensors to detect at least the temperature and pH of the dough, and fully programmable work-cycles that could be set in response to dough conditions.

In the countries I know best, Britain and the us, craft bakers are able to charge two to three times as much as industrial bakers for the same weight of bread. This clearly gives the craft bakers some latitude in production systems that industrial bakers don't have. Up to this point, the modern craft bakers almost all define themselves as not being industrial bakers. Most purposefully preserve traditions of handcraft, defining themselves in part by the fact that their loaves are touched by human hands, although machines that scale and form loaves are not unknown in artisan bakeries. But artisan

Wonder Bread made with 'Whole Grain White', USA.

bakers could redefine their relationship with the dough. In the world of art there are artists who are exhibited in the world's most prestigious museums who don't actually physically make their own work, but rather commission it. Perhaps we see this other approach beginning to develop in artisan bakeries that have grown to industrial scale, such as the La Brea Bakery in the US.

Each of the two commercial baking traditions – the craft baker and the industrial baker – play different cultural roles. Craft bakers, and particularly those who are critically acclaimed, are embedded in elite culinary culture. If the culinary elite is interested in 'country' food, purity of ingredients, concepts of authenticity where authenticity means roots in a European, or even more specifically in a French or Italian culinary dream of a village baker, then the elite craft bakers will craft breads to fit those interests. As the Hearthland Mill, a respected American craft bakery, puts it, 'European brick oven, wood fire, organic flour, natural leaven, dedicated and skilled bakers: what more could you ask for in a bakery?' This formulation reflects deep cultural biases. The 'European' wood-fired oven, the organic flour, the 'natural' leaven and the skilled bakers who are implicitly working the dough with their own hands are not the only pathways to superior bread. It is a formulation that focuses on an idealized concept that modern industrial processes have no place in the making of bread. In spirit, it is similar to arguments against machine-made objects put forward in the nineteenth century that have been definitively answered by the many machine-made objects we use every day that combine beautiful design with elegant functionality and flawless craft.

Industrial bakeries do not speak for the culinary elite but they do democratize elite breads, offering similar styles but in cheaper versions, much as the ready-to-wear trade offers cheaper versions of designer clothing. They also produce utilitarian breads such as bread for sandwiches and toast and they are the suppliers of buns for hamburgers and hot dogs. They lead in the adoption of the latest knowledge in dough biochemistry and materials processing to the task of producing breads as efficiently as possible, which often means pushing dough as fast as dough can be pushed. They excel in using their relationships with the wheat industry and their knowledge of dough biochemistry to make breads that fit their customers' seemingly impossible demands, for example, wholewheat or multi-grain loaves with a light rather than a dense crumb. They have managed what must have been a dream of bakers for millennia – to make white breads that are not just white as snow but soft as velvet.

Industrial bakers have revolutionized the ancient craft of bread-making to produce inexpensive breads by the millions that embody contradictory cultural desires. Unfortunately, where industrial breads tend to fail their customers is with flavour, and sometimes even in the most basic aspects of bread craft. Too often expediency is the controlling concept.

On more than one occasion I have purchased industrial white breads that weren't properly mixed, so one could see a swirl pattern from the mixer inadvertently baked into the crumb. Industrial breads often have slight off-flavours, presumably from the speed of production and the mix of ingredients that only a chemist can comprehend without a reference manual. Historically, in the baking trade, speed has been the enemy of both craft and richly flavoured breads. I don't think we can expect industrial bakers to significantly slow down their production lines – the capital costs involved in their operations may preclude that – but I do think this century will at least offer them the option of combining a more profound understanding of the biology of dough with advances in material processing to create profoundly better quality products, and with no, or very few, non-food ingredients. In the increasing number of consulting contracts between respected craft bakers and industrial bakers we are beginning to see some of the ethos of craft baking being transferred to industrial processes.

As I've mentioned, most flavour and textural changes in bread is created through the agency of fermentation, which triggers cascades of biochemical activity in the dough. These activities interact with each other so the changes initiated in the dough are interdependent and thus unbelievably complicated. Historically, bakers worked empirically. They didn't understand what was going on in dough but rather nurtured their dough based on their experience with how it reacts to inputs, in much the same way a gardener nurtures plants. The shift that could occur in this century is from the baker as nurturer to the baker as the definitive director of the process. To some extent this change in attitude is what took place in industrial bakeries during the twentieth century. It is what enabled them to create what are, in historic terms, such strange breads. They took charge of the baking process to force it in ways it hadn't been forced before. But this was, and is, a crude forcing compared to what might be possible as this century unfolds.

An example, and one that doesn't entail any change in process, but that does draw on the Internet and potentially on biotechnology, would be a shift in the yeasts used by bakers. Bakers have tended to look to sourdough cultures rather than to yeast for flavour. But, given time, yeasts can create flavour in dough and this offers an easy area for exploration by bakers with an interest in bread flavour. Bread itself is a subtle food. Subtle changes can be big changes. Home bakers, for whom length of fermentation makes no difference, could easily become a locus of innovation in the introduction of new yeasts into the baking trade.

As we have mentioned earlier, yeast, the fermentation agent in most bread, wine and beer recipes, is the fungus *Saccharomyces cerevisiae*. The classification of strains of *S. cerevisiae* as 'bread yeast' is a recent phenomenon, the result of the industrialization of yeast production for the baking trade. Up to the nineteenth century all bakers obtained yeast from brewers so there was no 'bread yeast'. What we call bread yeast are simply strains of *S. cerevisiae* that have been selected by yeast manufacturers primarily for their ability to quickly produce large quantities of gas while fermenting the dough; in other words, yeast strains that rapidly make bread 'light', which is what their customers have tended to demand. Bread yeast manufacturers focus their yeast development on the twin issues of gas production and speed with variants to suit different technical requirements of the baking trade: for example, yeast that will do well in a sweet dough, yeast that will do well in a sugarless dough or yeast that will thrive if mixed in with the flour rather than with the water.

How differently the wine and beer industry thinks of their yeasts! Manufacturers of beer and wine yeasts all describe multiple varieties of yeast, each producing a slightly differently flavoured product with some, in the case of wine, tied to specific varieties of grape. The importance of yeast strain in producing different varieties of beer is made clear in the following description of a yeast for sale by the American firm, White Labs, their *Belgian Saison II* beer yeast.

> Saison strain with more fruity ester production than with wlp565. Moderately phenolic, with a clove-like characteristic in finished beer flavor and aroma.

Wouldn't it be lovely to be able to purchase a 'bread yeast' that offered a 'clove-like' aroma when the bread was toasted? Or another yeast to produce a slight hint of smoke that might make it the ideal yeast for the Italian grilled bread bruschetta? What if bakers and scientists were to collaborate on bespoke yeasts that focused on flavour development in the dough so that the breads in a bakery might for the first time be differentiated by subtleties of aroma – the roll with a hint of blackcurrant and thyme under an overlay of apple next to a roll made with the same recipe but a different yeast and thus yielding a different aroma. The technical challenge is to create yeasts that will produce flavours fairly quickly and that will withstand baking in the environment of a dough. These new varieties could be developed through traditional selection or possibly through biotechnology.

In the short term the Internet offers bakers vast catalogues of yeast strains used by brewers and wine makers for experimentation. As with so much of our current agricultural heritage commercial yeast strains are monocultures and have tended to make us think that yeasts must be used one strain at a time. In fact yeast strains can be mixed. Whether or not bakers will wake up one morning with the realization that there are thousands of potential yeast strains to experiment with, and whether larger bakeries might soon or even ever contact yeast scientists to see how existing strains might be improved to enhance a bread's flavour and aroma is something that I cannot say. But it is already clear that as the century progresses it will be ever easier to imagine a baker and a yeast scientist having this kind of conversation. However, this is just one of many potential changes that could come to breads in this century and, given the speed with which we can now all communicate with each other, what is unknown this year may be widely adopted in only a few years' time.

Looking forward I think there is no question that as the century progresses the industrial bakers will continue to study the relationships in dough fermentation between yeast, bacteria, enzymes and grain variety in their pursuit of their goals. And they will also refine their baking technology to more closely monitor what is happening within the dough and make changes to the dough environment in response to these changes. Home bakers and artisan bakers will continue to talk to each other and the wall that currently exists between most industrial bakers and most artisan bakers will erode to the benefit of both traditions. While most of us who bake bread are still mostly nurturers of our dough, essentially working blind as we are able to test little more than dough temperature, as the century unfolds I suspect that everyone who bakes bread will gain access to inexpensive devices that will tell us a great deal about the chemistry of our dough and that bread baking technique will evolve to take advantage of that information. While the new technologies won't be for everyone, they will enable those who are interested to have unparalleled control over the breads they produce.

Bread has an unusual place as both an important food and as an important product of Western civilization. While it is not the food we still rely on as a dietary staple, it is a food, an object and an idea so thoroughly woven into our culture that it cannot help but be caught up in cultural change. Though breads may seem to change slowly, the changes that have taken place over the last 40 years are unprecedented in their breadth and depth. Between the rapid advances we are seeing in areas of biotechnology and materials handling that touch on the baking trade, the revolutionary changes that continue to transform the way we communicate with and share complex information with each other, and what looks like a sustained revival of interest in the quality of the foods we eat, I think we can expect our bread culture to continue changing. There will be more edges than ever before – more interactions between ideas – and as bread is really nothing more than an idea for how to combine water, flour and leavening, the richer the intellectual interchange, the richer the bread culture will become. It is impossible to predict at the level of the loaf, but in general we are entering exciting times for bread bakers: a time when breads will develop in unpredictable, but genuinely interesting ways.

Recipes

These recipes illustrate breads mentioned in this book that are rarely documented in cookbooks or other collections of recipes. I join with many of my colleagues in the field of culinary history who believe it is helpful to get a feel for the history of food by actually getting into the kitchen. The recipes are written with the assumption that you already know how to bake bread. If you have technical questions, consult a friend, any of the many wonderful bread books that have been published recently or websites devoted to bread-making. I often find my technical questions answered by videos posted to Internet video sites like YouTube.

Flour: As bakers we are lucky. Our flour is of consistent quality. We do not have to worry about making bread from grains that sprouted in the field, moulded in storage or were badly damaged by insects before milling. We also don't have to make bread with local grains that may not be best for making loaf breads. The flour we buy always shows breads off to great advantage. Besides issues of consistency, which are all in our favour, the greatest difference between modern flour and the best bread flours used by bakers prior to the industrial revolution is that in the past bakers prized fresh flour while today's bakers prize flour that has been aged at least six weeks. Furthermore, much of the flour purchased in shops by home bakers is much older than a few weeks and is often stale. While our breads always look the best they can, they may not taste as good as they could. You can greatly increase the

Bread oven in front of labourers' huts, Mexico, *c.* 1914.

flavour of the breads you bake by using flour that is freshly milled. This is particularly true for any flour that retains some or all of its bran.

Historically, only the poorest of the poor made breads with wholemeal flour. For the sake of authenticity it is usually advisable to at least sift out the larger pieces of bran, whether you purchase your flour or mill your own. When buying wholemeal flour I suggest buying the coarsest grind because its bran will be in larger pieces and easier to sift out.

Mixing containers: Wooden troughs or barrels were the standard mixing containers for bread. While they were scraped out after use, they were never completely cleaned. Thus, each batch of bread helped inoculate the next, even if no other starter was added. If you don't have a wooden bowl you can use, consider dedicating a ceramic or metal bowl to bread-making that can always be left with a little dried bread dough in it to help inoculate the next batch. This can improve bread flavour even when making yeasted dough.

Yeast: Until the development of factory-produced yeast in the nineteenth century bakers obtained yeast from the brewer. Barm, the yeast-laden sediment thrown off in the ale brewing process, is preferred for all yeasted bread recipes that date prior to the later decades of the nineteenth century. Some degree of hop flavour, even if not obviously detectable, was present in most yeasted breads for at least 300 years. By using real ale barm you put that flavour back. Brewers are usually happy to give you barm if you bring the jar. Use five to eight times the amount of barm, by weight, that the recipe calls for in dried yeast. Thus if a recipe calls for 7 g (one packet) dried yeast, use 35–55 g (1.25–2 oz) barm. If ale is heavily hopped the barm can be too bitter to use without washing. Wash barm by pouring off the liquid above the sediment, replace with plentiful distilled water, stir, let the yeast settle out, pour off the water and repeat.

Cake yeast usually gives bread a rich, warm taste. Of the dried yeasts, try to avoid 'instant' yeasts that also contain dough conditioners – read labels. See pp. 128–9 for ideas on using beer and wine yeasts. The dried yeast specified in these recipes is the non-instant variety.

Ovens: Most of these breads were baked in wood-fired ovens made of clay, brick or stone. Oven doors were often hermetically sealed with wet clay or a mix of ash and grease so the interior of the ovens was steamy during baking from water that evaporated from the baking dough. Commercial bread ovens often include systems for introducing steam into the baking chamber. Sustained steam is hard to recreate in a home oven.

If possible, bake on a baking stone. This improves the bottom crust.

Because the fire is swept out of a wood-fired oven before use, bread was historically baked in a falling oven. I replicate the falling oven in a few of the recipes by suggesting that you lower the oven temperature after the bread has started baking.

Unleavened Flatbread: Griddle or Ember Baked

Based on today's archaeology, flatbreads made with bread grains were known at least 20,000 years ago and flatbreads made with other types of starches can be traced back even further in time.

While there is no prescribed size, a disc 10–12 cm (4–5 inches) in diameter is always manageable, as is a thickness of 3–6 mm (⅛–¼ inches). When made of wheat and baked on a hot surface, like glowing embers, this bread often puffs up into a ball while baking and may thus be hollow in the centre. Thicker or thinner breads produce different taste and texture profiles.

Contrary to the intuition of those of us who cook on gas or electric stoves rather than open fires, a bed of glowing embers makes the perfect surface on which to bake flatbreads: the ash doesn't stick, the bread doesn't burn and the resulting product is indistinguishable from one baked in a hot wood-fired oven. The Old and New Testaments, as well as the Talmud, have many references to breads or 'cakes' baked on the embers. See the King James translation of the New Testament, John 21:9, for mention of ember-baked breads.

Because the baker doesn't manipulate the dough with fermentation, unleavened flatbreads are entirely dependent on the flour for taste. You will be rewarded if you can make this flatbread with fresh flour. It is implicit in Homer that it was the practice in Ancient Greece to grind the flour on the day the breads were to be baked, a standard practice today in villages in northern India, such as those in Rajasthan.

Add to 1 kg (2½ lb) wheat or barley flour of any degree of refinement enough water to form a moderately stiff dough. Knead until smooth. Form into a ball, cover and allow to rest for 20 minutes. Form into balls 100–150 g (4–6 oz) each, roll into thin discs and bake one of two ways. Either bake on a hot griddle to set the dough and then finish directly over a gas burner or on a bed of glowing hardwood embers, turning frequently so steam will force the dough to puff up, perhaps even to puff up into a ball, or bake in a hot (370–400°C/700–750°F) wood-fired oven, turning as soon as the dough is set and then turning as needed both to create steam within the bread and to prevent it from burning. When done, breads should have small brown markings and even a few spots of burn. As the breads are finished, pile them on a plate and optionally brush with clarified butter (ghee) in the modern North

Indian fashion. If the breads don't puff up at all then either they are too thick or the embers or oven not hot enough.

Note: Flatbreads can also be leavened and baked the same way as unleavened breads. Yeast and sourdough are both appropriate leavenings for flatbreads, each with their own ancient traditions.

Flatbreads from pulses: broad (fava) beans, field peas and chick peas

Pulses were domesticated around the same time as grains. For those who couldn't afford breads from grains, pulses were a common flatbread alternative – the first step up the hierarchical bread ladder. Breads made with non-grain starches pre-date grain breads so in a sense pulse breads are part of the oldest bread tradition. Pulse flatbreads are now so far removed from the European flatbread tradition that, except for the revival of a batter-baked flatbread made of chickpeas in parts of Northern Italy (*torta di ceci*) and adjacent parts of France (*socca*), pulse flatbreads are no longer part of Europe's bread tradition, which is too bad because they can be delicious. The primary technical difficulty working with pulse flour is being sure that the flour cooks thoroughly. Pea flour can be ground from any dried pea; it was a field pea that was used for *pease meal* rather than the green pea that is most easily purchased dried in our groceries.

In my experience, if you can grind the flour for your own pulse breads you will be richly rewarded with a fresher, brighter flavour than that obtained from packaged flour. If grinding your own, sift out the larger pieces of bran, if any. Chickpea flour is widely available in groceries but outside India, where pulse flatbreads remain popular, the best commercial source for flour from pulses is groceries catering to Indian immigrant communities. Pulse breads taste very different depending on the pulse flour used.

There is good documentation from northern England, Scotland and Ireland up to the mid-nineteenth century for flatbreads made from a mix of pulse flour and a largely unrefined grain flour, such as barley, rye or wheat. A stiff batter rolled thinly produces a lovely cracker. Thicker, and one has a rustic bannock or scone. For this mixed flour variant I suggest a ratio of 1:1 pulse to grain flour.

Mix enough water with 500 g (17 oz) dried pea, chickpea or fava bean flour to make a stiff paste. Water may be cold, hot or even boiling. If using boiling water, mix with a wooden spoon. Let dough rest for 20 minutes and then adjust liquid if too stiff to handle. Form into balls 100–150 g (4–6 oz) each, use your hands to press into discs and then roll thinly. Bake on a moderately hot dry griddle until the cake is thoroughly cooked. Thicker breads can be baked directly in hot ashes or wrapped in large leaves like those of the cabbage family. The delicious *torta di ceci* of today's Italy is made with a batter of chickpea flour poured into a hot frying pan over a liberal quantity of almost smoking olive oil. If imagining a similar batter-bread from a more northerly area in Europe then use a fat appropriate to the region (cow, pig, chicken or dripping). Turn when set. Thick pulse breads are best eaten hot.

Loaf breads adulterated with pulse flour

In Europe pea and bean flours were used to stretch (adulterate) loaf breads. As pulses were added for economic reasons, they were probably mixed with grain flour that was minimally refined. Though information is scarce there is one published recipe indicating that pea flour was mixed with water just off the boil before adding to the bread grains. The proportions for this recipe, 1:4 pea to rye flour, are derived from Henry Best's *Farming and Memorandum Book* of 1641 (see pp. 45, 46, 54). Until modern times late spring was often a time of food scarcity in the countryside as winter reserves were used up but crops weren't ready for harvest. Pulse-adulterated breads were a means to cover for a shortfall in the family's store of grain. In this case, if the family always cut the bread with 25 per cent pea flour it was equivalent to adding three month's worth of grain to the household's grain inventory. The method for mixing the bread roughly follows that of the Brown Bread described by Gervase Markham in *The English Housewife* (1615).

This bread is made with 100 g (3½ oz) pea flour and 400 g (14 oz) rye flour. If doing your own grinding sift out the larger pieces of bran. Mix with 350 g (12 oz) water to form a stiff dough and an optional 5 g (teaspoon) salt. Bring the water to the boil and then pour over the pea flour. Stir with a wooden spoon until mixed, add the salt, stir and allow to stand for a few minutes. While still hot add the rye flour and mix thoroughly. When cool enough to handle wet your hands and work the dough until it is thoroughly mixed, smooth and satiny. (If working a large amount of dough, work over the dough with clenched fists kept wet as necessary to prevent sticking.) Cover, and let sour in a warm place, usually 24–36 hours. If not soured, leave longer or add a little yeast. Form into a single large loaf and let rise for four hours. Rye dough doesn't rise so much as get softer. Place on a floured peel and slide onto a baking stone in a preheated oven set to 230°C (400°F) for one hour, and then lower to 175°C (350°F) until the interior temperature measures 93.3°C (200°F) on an instant-read thermometer, an additional one to two hours. If you bake directly on a metal tray, oil it first. Larger loaves could take as long as six hours to bake. In case of doubt always let the bread bake longer. When done, remove from the oven and cool bottom side up. Wait one to two days before slicing.

Basic Horse-bread

This is a bread for horses but was also eaten by the poor and more generally in times of dearth. For the best flavour acquire bran for the bread by sifting it out of wholemeal flour that you milled yourself. For the next best flavour acquire the bran by sifting it from flour you buy. It is possible to purchase bran but that bran is purer than what one sifts oneself. It behaves differently from home-produced product.

To 250 g (9 oz) bran from wheat, rye or barley add 250 g (9 oz) water. Let the bran sit for 20 minutes to absorb water, and then add enough rye flour (and additional water if needed) so the bran will stick together, 150–250 g (5–9 oz). Knead until well mixed and the dough begins to feel gelatinously slippery. The bread can be baked immediately when being fed to a horse but, if you plan on eating it, the flavour will be improved by letting the dough sour, a suggestion offered by the publisher John Hougton in the late seventeenth century. To sour, allow to rest for twelve to 48 hours. Form into a thin loaf, rest it for a couple of hours and then place on a floured peel and slide onto a baking stone in a preheated moderate oven and bake until done. This is a delicious speciality bread that can be used in lieu of German pumpernickel on the hors-d'oeuvre table.

Rye Bread

For many hundreds of years, rye was the second most important bread grain in Europe after wheat. It was also an important grain in North America well into the nineteenth century. The bread we now think of as 'Russian rye' was well known throughout much of Europe. Rye produces breads that range from the blackest black and if refined to a white nearly as white as wheat flour. While rye does contain gluten, the chemistry of rye leavening is different from that of wheat flour. The gas-trapping structures are triggered by souring, so 100 per cent rye breads are always sour-leavened. Rye bread made with a highly refined rye flour does display 'eyes' similar to those of wheat breads, but as a rule rye breads rarely have discernible air holes in the crumb. Rye dough sours more readily than does a dough made with wheat flour and thus does not require the introduction of a starter to the dough. The taste of the final bread can range from sweet to intensely sour depending on how the dough is handled. This recipe tends to produce a sweet-tasting bread as the hot wet initial fermentation favours lactobacillus over bacteria that produce a more acidic environment.

In European winters rye bread was often mixed with water just off the boil and then covered with a cloth to keep it warm. The recipe I offer here is based on the faithfully accurate ethnography of

Marcel Maget, who in the 1950s documented the annually baked rye bread of the French alpine village Villar d'Arène. You may use a wholegrain rye flour, but if you imagine yourself to have had a reasonably prosperous year on your farm then sift out at least the biggest pieces of bran. This bread was intended for long keeping and does not contain salt.

The dough is made with 1 kg (2½ lb) rye flour and 600 g (21 oz) water just off the boil. Put one third of the flour (333 g/12 oz) in a bowl and from shoulder height pour the hot water over it. Use a wooden spoon or spatula to thoroughly mix and then wrap the bowl in a blanket and keep at 22°C (72°F) until it begins to sour, usually between twelve and 24 hours. Once the batter begins to ferment, use your hands to mix in the rest of the flour (666 g/ 24 oz). Rye dough is sticky. Once thoroughly mixed, clean your hands, and now with wet hands knead a few times until smooth and satiny. (If working a large amount of dough, work over the dough with clenched fists kept wet to prevent sticking.) Let sit covered for a further 12 hours, form into a single 1 kg (2½ lb) loaf and let rest in a warm place for two to four hours before baking. Follow the baking procedures for the pea/rye bread recipe. Let the bread rest for at least 24 hours and preferably for two days before cutting. The flavour improves for at least two weeks. If you make a large loaf (for example, 5 kg/12½ lb), cut some of it in tranches to dry and then chip into pieces and rehydrate to consume as a cold porridge or in soup.

Maslin Bread

For centuries, maslin bread, usually a mix of rye and wheat, *meteil* in French, was the dominant bread of the Northern European countryside. Versions of maslin breads were widely appreciated for their fine flavour. Since combinations of the grain ratio, degree of flour refinement and leavening systems are essentially without limit, maslin bread offers a lifetime of experimentation. In the eighteenth century the French had names for different types of *meteil* flour based on the ratios of rye to wheat: *grande meteil* (2:1), *meteil* (1:1) and *ble ramé* (1:8). The less refined, and the higher the percentage of rye, the denser the bread. The higher the percentage of wheat the less need there is to sour the dough, thus a bread made with *meteil* or *ble ramé* can be leavened with yeast. *Ble ramé* includes rye in a ratio that is often found in modern recipes for *pain de campagne*.

Make a moderately stiff dough with 1 kg (2½ lb) *meteil* flour (1:1 rye to wheat), 600–650 g (21–23 oz) room-temperature water, 10 g (2 tsp) salt and 7 g (2 tsp) non-instant dried yeast. Rehydrate with some of the water. Mix all the ingredients, knead, let rise for at least four to five hours (it will become softer and if you cut into it with a sharp knife there will be small air holes, but it will not double), gently de-gas, form into loaves, let these prove until they have begun to rise again, then place on a floured peel and slide onto a baking stone in a preheated oven set to 220°C (425°F) for 15 minutes, and then lower the oven to 190°C (350°F) until the interior temperature reaches 93°C (200°F), around 1.5 hours. If you bake on a metal tray, oil it first. Larger loaves may take longer. Remove from the oven and let cool bottom side up. Allow to rest one day before cutting.

Manchet

This is a very important white bread. While the name is English, the style, a white bread with a dough that was dense enough to knead with one's feet or a brake – a pole attached to a wall by a pivot and worked over the dough until it oxidized – was a common elite bread at least during the first few hundred years of the modern era and probably long before. In France open-crumbed crisp-crusted breads, like the modern baguette, probably began replacing this style bread in the early 1600s and were presumably formulated as the not-manchet. In many ways the manchet is very much with us by its demonstrable absence from most of our bread choices.

As with modern breads, like the baguette, there is no one recipe for a manchet. Each of the few published English recipes in the 1500 and 1600s is different, though each achieves a result that was accepted as a manchet because what makes a manchet a manchet is not the leavening system, nor the recipe's structure; rather it is the basic relationship between water and flour, the way it is kneaded, the way it is baked, and probably also the shape of the loaf, although there isn't enough documentary evidence to prove this hunch right. The recipe I offer here uses the structure of the most well known of these recipes, that of Gervase Markham, published in *The English Housewife* (1615).

Since manchet is not made from a dough that is currently popular in Britain or North America, few readers will have experience with a bread of this type, even those who bake often. What you should do is keep good notes on what you do. In particular keep track of how much water you add to the flour because it is here that you will have to make adjustments to get a final loaf that is worthy of an Elizabethan table. For this bread there is a fine line between a dough that is too stiff and one that is too slack. The crumb can be dense but not so dense that it reminds one of a dense brown bread. Throughout the early twentieth century British bread recipes called for 50 per cent water by weight of flour. That is the basic ratio for historic manchet recipes but many modern flours absorb more water than did flours of the early modern period, so you may need more water to achieve the same result. The bread in the painting *Still-life with a Chessboard* (1630) by Lubin Baugin (see p. 40) is a manchet-style bread, though the shape is different from what seems to have been most common in England. The bread should come out of the oven looking very white – like a par-baked loaf. Historically, this bread was usually leavened with beer barm and in my experience using barm offers better flavour than commercial bread yeast.

To 1 kg (2½ lb) unbleached white flour add 10 g (2 tsp) salt, 550 g (19 oz) warm water and 7 g (2 tsp) non-instant dried yeast, rehydrated with some of the water. If using barm then use about 35–58 g (2½–4 tbsp). After forming into a dough, turn out onto a work table. Knead as much as possible by hand and then repeatedly work over the dough with a long thin rolling pin or a 2.5 cm (1 inch) dowel by pressing it deeply into the dough and then refolding the dough on top of itself as it spreads until you feel the dough change and become smooth, satiny and stretchy-elastic. You may not notice it but the dough should oxidize while being mixed and thus get a little whiter. This may take some time. Form into a ball, cover and set aside until the dough doubles in bulk. When risen, gently press out the gas and form into two equal-sized balls. Gently flatten. With a razor or sharp knife make an incision around the disc's waist. Using a pointed knife poke at least six holes in the bread's top, then immediately place on a peel and slide onto a baking stone in a preheated oven set to 135°C (275°F) and bake for approximately one hour. The bread will rise but the crust should not brown. Serve the following day.

Pain de mie
White Loaf Bread

The modern white sandwich loaf, staple of industrial bakeries, is the direct heir to millennia of enriched breads destined for elite tables. While the whiteness and softness of the modern industrial loaf may represent the *reductio ad absurdum* of democratized elite taste, the modern artisan baker's form of the industrial white sandwich bread – a yeasted white loaf enriched with milk and sometimes a little butter – is easily traced to published recipes for breads that were classified in eighteenth- and early nineteenth-century France as a fashionable bread, a *pain à la mode*. The recipe offered here is the *pain à la Montoron* by Louis Liger, published in the 1711 edition of *Maison rustique*. If possible use raw full fat milk for this recipe as the fat content and bacterial flora in raw milk are factors in precisely reproducing this bread. This same dough can also be formed into rolls.

Measure out 500 g (1 lb) flour. Take a quarter of that flour, 125 g (4 oz), and mix it with 130 g (4½ oz) milk at blood heat, 4 g (1 tsp) non-instant dried yeast rehydrated with some of the milk, and 7 g (1½ tsp) salt. Cover and set aside in a warm place for an hour. Mix into this starter the remaining flour and enough water (approximately 190 g/5½–7 oz), also at blood heat, to form a soft dough. Mix just enough to form into a homogeneous mass but do not knead. Divide into loaves, allow to rise in wooden bowls dusted with flour. Turn out onto a peel and slide onto a baking stone in a preheated moderate oven. Bake until done, approximately one hour.

Chipped Bread and Rasped Rolls

This is not a recipe for a bread or a roll. Rather, it is a description of how breads and rolls for elite tables (and tables that aspired to be elite) were prepared for consumption after baking. As evidenced from many sources, including cookbooks and literary texts, for many centuries European and at least some North American elite diners eschewed crust, instead preferring to eat breads and rolls that had crusts chipped or later rasped off when the breads were still hot. Thus chipping or rasping breads is assumed in most early modern bread recipes (1500–1800), and can also be assumed for many breads well into the nineteenth century, even in North America. For example, most editions of Mary Randolph's *The Virginia Housewife*, one of the most popular cookbooks prior to the American Civil War (1860), specify that 'bread must be rasped when baked'. The last published recipe for rasped rolls that is in the widely read twentieth-century American cookbook by Fanny Farmer, *The Boston Cooking-School Cookbook* (1924) under the name 'Rasped Roll'. Chipping and rasping offers an unlimited source of breadcrumbs for use in cooking and is the source of the breadcrumbs so often referenced in early cookbooks.

Chipping means just that. When the bread is still hot use a knife to chip off the crust. Since crust was considered hard to digest, chipping (and depth of chipping), was in part a medicinal step and thus was determined, in part, by a sense of the health of the diner. This was probably true at least up to the eighteenth century. For the modern chipper let aesthetics be your guide. To find the perfect chipping knife you may need to work through your knife collection to find the ideal mix of sharpness and weight. To make rasped rolls bake rolls in a hot oven until the crust is deep brown. A rasp is not a grater. Purchase a rasp from your local hardware store. While the rolls are still hot, rasp off the brown colour so the roll turns pale. Some bakers baked rolls until they were dark brown, even nearly burnt, to facilitate chipping and rasping, a practice that I recommend. Fanny Farmer instructs that the rasped rolls be put back in the hot oven for a further five minutes. This re-baking further crisps the remaining now rasped crust and repairs damage where one has rasped through to the crumb. There is not enough evidence to tell whether this was a standard practice after rasping or a novel instruction possibly to cover for technical errors by bakers no longer experienced in rasping rolls. You will find that the visual and textural effect of rasping rolls is well worth the effort. One way in which rasped rolls were served was in the fold of the white linen napkin at each place setting. Use the recipe for *Pain de Mie*, above, or any recipe for a white roll that is not so enriched it will not reliably form a deep crust.

Glossary

Ash cakes (International): A flatbread, usually unleavened, made with any type of flour at hand. This includes the flour of grains, pulses and tree nuts, especially chestnut and acorn. The breads are formed into a small, flat cake baked within a mix of ash and embers in the fireplace or campfire. Sometimes ash cakes are baked wrapped in large leaves, such as cabbage or banana. Historically a common bread of the very poor, the dispossessed, defeated armies and fugitives, such as the escaped American slave Frederick Douglass.

Bagel (American/International): The bagel, originally of European origin, was modified in America to its present form, which is generally thicker than its European antecedents, such as Polish exemplars. It was originally associated with Jewish culture in New York but is now one of the most popular American breads. The bagel is a roll formed into a circle and boiled before baking. Traditionally it is both fine-grained and chewy. Industrial bagels may not be boiled and may have a soft crumb. Today bagels are frequently baked with a variety of toppings such as poppy seed, sesame and onion and are often cut in half and served with butter, cream cheese or other spreads such as hummus. In the US they are often served with smoked salmon at Sunday brunch.

Baguette (French/International): One of the most internationally recognized French breads. It is defined more by its shape and crust than by any one recipe. The standard baguette is a long thin white bread with a crispy, crackly crust marked with diagonal slash patterns, but the baguette is changing and both the slash pattern and dough type are in flux. Baguettes that are not entirely white are increasingly common, even in Paris. Most bakeries in France have a selection of nearly burnt baguettes that you can ask for as *bien cuit*, well cooked. The standard baguette is 5–6 cm (2–2½ inches) in diameter and about 65 cm (24 inches) long.

Bannock (British and Irish): The general name for a griddle-baked hearth bread that is often made with barley flour. Now usually leavened with baking powder or soda.

Barley bread (British): A traditional country loaf common in many parts of England up to the mid-nineteenth century. Barley bread was often baked as a *boule*, but is now usually baked in a tin. It is usually yeast leavened and historically often made with skimmed milk.

Bâtard (French): An oval loaf, usually 500 g–1 kg (17 oz–2½ lb), and usually made with white flour. No one recipe is associated with the shape. The classic *bâtard* is hand-shaped by the baker and baked on the floor of the oven rather than in a tin or on a mesh screen.

Blini (Russia, Belarus, Lithuania and adjacent regions/International): A thick sourdough or yeast-leavened pancake made with wheat, buckwheat or rye flour and traditionally used as a staple bread in the countryside. It has a long tradition as an appetizer at high-status meals in the form of small white flour pancakes served with caviar.

Bloomer (British): A traditional white bread, typically baked in a *bâtard* shape and with diagonal slashes cut into the top crust.

Bolillo (Mexico/Regional USA): The Mexican-Spanish name for a classic European white roll. Sold in many forms, a common one is with a single slash down the middle of a crisp-crusted *bâtard*-shaped roll.

Boston brown bread (American): Made with a mix of wheat, corn, and often rye and also often with molasses, 'Brown Bread', with and without molasses was a common bread in nineteenth-century New England. The identification of the molasses variant with Boston is fairly recent. The modern form is usually steamed rather than baked, usually includes raisins, but rarely includes the nineteenth-century rye, and may be leavened with baking powder. Now rare.

Boule (French): A round loaf, usually 500 g–1 kg (17 oz–2 ½ lb), but sometimes much larger. In France a common shape for *pain de campagne,* but no one recipe is associated with the shape. The classic *boule* is hand-shaped by the baker and baked on the floor of the oven rather than in a tin or on a mesh screen.

Brezel/Laugenbrezel (German/International): Brezelen (pretzels) are always baked in the unique Brezel shape, a distinctive form that in many languages lives as a shape independent of the bread. The Brezel shape is formed by rolling the yeasted dough into a long snake twisted in the middle to form three distinct lobes, the overall outside of the shape more or less forming a heart shape. **Laugenbrezel** are boiled in lye to produce the shiny deep-brown crust.

Brioche (French/International): In France the brioche is referred to as a *gateau* or cake rather than a bread. The white wheat dough is highly enriched with butter and egg. It is sold in the form of small rolls, usually baked in a fluted mould, and also in the form of a loaf, usually around 500 g (17 oz), either baked in the same fluted shape as the small rolls, or in the form of a sandwich loaf.

Broa (Portugal/International): A leavened corn bread, often a mix of corn and rye.

Brötchen (German): 'Little bread' – the general name for German rolls. There is a vast world of German rolls, as all German bread doughs can be scaled down to roll-size. As a rule German rolls are baked in the round (*boule*) or long (*bâtard*) shapes. Brezelen, both hard and soft, are also classified as *Brötchen*.

Brown bread (British): Historically a bread made with flour that retained enough bran to make the bread brown, also a comparatively coarse bread made from a mix of grains. Today often made with wholemeal flour and usually baked in a tin. However, there is no legal definition of 'brown bread' and it may include white flour and get some of the brown colour from malt or brown sugar.

Challah (European Jewish/International): This bread is associated with the start of the Jewish Sabbath, Friday evening, and is thus more frequently available in bakeries on Fridays. It is a lightly enriched white bread that always includes eggs, and may include saffron which lend it a yellow cast. It is baked in the form of a braided or plaited *bâtard*; the number of braids may range from three to many. Often glazed with egg and dusted with poppy seeds.

Chapatti (India/International): There are many forms of chapatti, the staple flatbread of northern South Asia. The most basic version from Rajasthan is an unleavened bread made with wheat flour, though not necessarily white flour, usually 15–18 cm (6–7 inches) in diameter. When made at home it is first baked on the concave side of the *tava*, a curved griddle, before being finished on embers or directly over the flame of a gas burner.

Cheat (English): This is the historic term for a large range of household breads that were less than white, or made with a mix of wheat and other flours, such as wheat and rye (also called maslin) or wheat and barley. In terms of refinement, between a refined white loaf and a coarser brown loaf.

Ciabatta (Italian/International): A white bread made with a dough that is so hydrated it is almost a batter. Characterized by large irregular air holes and a squat rectilinear shape. The dough usually contains olive oil. This is currently one of the most popular international breads. When used, it displaces the baguette.

Conchas (Mexico/Regional USA): One of the more colourful types of *pan dulce*. A sweet, yeasted milk roll topped with a granular and often coloured frosting that is distinctively marked with fine wire cutters to form complex swirling patterns often reminiscent of scallops and other sea shells.

Cornbread (American): The modern American version of cornbread usually includes some sugar and is often baked in a square loaf tin or in the form of American muffins. There are many regional American versions, most of which are associated with the American South.

Cottage loaf (British): A white bread with a round base and a topknot. A British classic, but increasingly rare.

Crescentine (Italy, Modenese mountains region): A leavened flatbread roughly 10 cm (4 inches) in diameter baked sandwiched between tiles (*tigelle*) heated in the embers of the fireplace. They are classically baked in a stack of these tiles in front of the fireplace, sometimes with chestnut leaves between the dough and the tile. Now often baked on electric griddles.

Croissant (French/International): Not a bread but a classic of the bakers art of Viennoiserie, a large class of fat and also sometimes sugar-enriched pastries. The croissant is a 'laminated dough'. It is made from a yeast dough layered with butter and repeatedly folded and rolled out to create a rough puff pastry. Always shaped as a crescent, hence its name. A staple of the 'Continental breakfast'.

Crumpets (British/International): One of a class of northern English and Scottish griddle breads that includes other breads, such as the pikelet. Crumpets sit on the cusp between bread and pancake. Baked on one side, the top is a mass of small air holes that reach to the bottom crust. Traditionally toasted in front of an open fire, spread with butter and jam and eaten hot.

Ficelle (French): A long, thin loaf made with **baguette** dough, about half the width of a baguette, and as long.

Fougasse (French): This is a wheat bread that can have as many shapes as there are bakeries that produce it. It is said to derive from a hearth bread, like pizza. So many different breads go under the name fougasse that what it refers to has more to do with local custom than a recipe. In one common form it is a bread dough mixed with savoury ingredients like olive, onion or tomato and baked as a large, thin cake out of which pieces are cut.

French roll (American): A lightly enriched white roll often served at formal meals.

Fry bread (Native American): A leavened bread, though the leavening can be baking powder, usually enriched with milk rolled thinly and fried in oil. In one form or another it is now widely associated with Native American tribes including the Seminole, Navajo, Creek, Chickasaw, Blackfeet and Cherokee. It is always encountered at festivals.

Graham bread (American): This is the same as wholewheat bread. It was popularized by Sylvester Graham, an influential early nineteenth-century proponent of wholegrain flour. It is usually sold as a sandwich bread. One more commonly sees 'Graham Flour' for sale than 'Graham Bread'.

Host (Roman Catholic/International): A thin round unleavened wafer made from the finest white flour blessed by a priest during the communion ceremony of transubstantiation, usually stamped with a religious symbol.

Ingera (Ethiopia and Eritria/International): A large, sour fermented pancake baked on one side, like the crumpet, made with *teff*, a small black grain. The finished bread covers the serving plate, food is placed on top and diners use their hands to eat the meal, including the bread, which is sometimes used to grasp the food.

Khobz (Morocco/France): A mould-baked yeast or sourdough bread. It can be made from wholemeal or refined flours including mixes of flour such as wheat, semolina, corn or barley. If made from semolina it is called *khobz dyal smida*. A common form today is round and a few centimetres thick. Often flavoured with sesame and anise.

Knäckebröd (Swedish, regional under different names/International): A crisp rye bread baked in the form of a disk with a hole in the centre, originally so the bread could be baked in quantity and stored on a pole set high in the kitchen. Often elaborately stamped, this style of bread is widespread in Scandinavia with different names for the bread in the different Scandinavian languages. Widely available packaged outside its region of origin.

Kümmelstange (German): A thick bread stick often glazed and sprinkled with caraway seeds and salt. A typical form is 8 x 2 cm (3 x 1 inches) and a little narrower at each end.

Kürbiskernbrot (German): Pumpkin seed bread. Usually a *Mehrkornbrot* (multi-grain) or *Mischbrot* (rye wheat mix) with pumpkin seeds in the dough and on the exterior.

Laufabrauð (Iceland, seasonal): One of the most beautiful breads (see p. 74). A thin crisp white flatbread rolled as thin as a leaf, incised with delicate patterns, such as a snowflake, ice crystals or a star-studded night, and fried. A traditional Christmas bread.

Lauganbrezel (Germany/International): see under **Brezel**.

Lavash (Iran, Armenia, Georgia and Azerbaijan/International): A large oval unleavened tandoor-baked flatbread, now made with white flour. Usually crisp when cool.

Leinsamenbrot (German): Linseed bread. Usually a *Mehrkornbrot* (multi-grain) or *Mischbrot* (rye wheat mix) with linseeds in the dough and on the exterior.

Manaqish bi'l Za'atar (Lebanon, Palestine and region): Manakish is a generic name for a widely loved pizza-like bread. The underlying dough can be the same as that used to make pitta. Like pizza, after forming the final flatbread, it is spread with a topping like chilli, minced lamb, cheese or in this case *za'atar*, an aromatic mix of local wild herbs that usually includes varieties of oregano, basil thyme (Calamintha species), thyme and savory, and is often mixed with sesame sees, dried sumac, salt and other spices.

Maslin (English): This is the historic term for a bread made with a mix of flours but usually denoted a mix of wheat and rye. Roughly synonymous with the French *meteil* and the German *Mischbrot*.

Matzo (Jewish/International): The primary Jewish flatbread. The modern version is an unleavened thin fine wheat cracker punched with many small holes to keep it from rising. Now mostly an industrial bread sold in boxes as a square cracker to suit the convenience of the industrial baker.

Mehrkornbrot (German): Multi-grain bread. Sold in a plethora of shapes, grain mixtures and often with seeds on the outside.

Meteil (French): Equivalent to the English maslin, usually refers to an equal mix of wheat and rye. This mix was so common in eighteenth-century France it was treated as a third bread grain; grain markets quoted for *meteil* alongside wheat and rye.

Miche (French): Usually refers to a round loaf or *boule* and can be made with any bread dough.

Mischbrot (German): This is the European classic rye/wheat mix. In English the less precise term is maslin. More closely similar to the French *meteil* because it suggests a 1:1 ratio of rye to wheat. See also Roggenmischbrot and Weizenmischbrot.

Mohnbrötchen (Germany): Poppy seed roll. May have a pattern, like a star, cut into the top crust. Often similar to the *Sesambrötchen*.

Muffin (English): A yeasted griddle-baked bread. The dough is rolled out to approximately 1 cm (½ inch), cut in rounds a few centimetres across and baked. When cool it is traditionally divided in half with the tines of a fork creating a rough surface. The bread is then toasted (re-baked) and served hot, usually with butter and marmalade or jam. This is the muffin so often referred to in Charles Dickens's novels.

Müslibrötchen (German): A roll inspired by muesli cereal. Oats on top, and often with raisins within.

Naan (Northern India and adjacent regions/International): In terms of this large region, a general name for a leavened flatbread. Usually baked in a tandoor oven. Common in Indian restaurants. There are many variants of naan, garlic naan being a popular restaurant offering. Now made with white flour. Generally softer and lighter than the unleavened chapatti.

Pain à l'ancienne (French): The best translation is 'traditional bread'. As a rule, if you have to declare something traditional, it probably isn't. Bakeries use the name to imply an older production system with comparatively long rising times. It is usually a white bread that is often, but not always, leavened with sourdough (*levain*).

Pain aux olives/lardon/figue/etc. (French): Breads that have an ingredient mixed in. These are often sold in the form of rolls and are also often made with at least some wholewheat flour to suggest rustic origins. These types of breads were known in the ancient world.

Pain bouilli (French Alps): A 100 per cent rye bread from the French Alps. Mixed with water just off the boil, this bread was traditionally baked once a year in large rectangular loaves, usually in November, and then eaten throughout the year, mostly as a dried bread that required rehydrating to be palatable.

Pain complet (French): Wholegrain, usually wheat, a 'complete' loaf.

Pain de campagne (French/International): Literally bread of the countryside; there is no single recipe. The bread usually has a 'rustic' component in the form of wholewheat flour, rye flour or both. It is never baked in a tin, is usually very crusty, usually baked as a *boule* and can range in size up to several kilograms. As a rule, it is a sourdough or *levain*-leavened bread. It has an international following.

Pain de mie (French): A lightly enriched white sandwich bread baked in a loaf tin with a lid, which prevents the formation of a top crust. The primary difference between the French *pain de mie* and similar white sandwich breads sold in the UK and the USA is that there is no sugar in this dough.

Pan dulce (Mexico/Regional USA): A class of sweet bread that includes a variety of dough types and bread shapes, some soft, like *conchas*, and some hard and pastry-like like the laminated palmier-class *orejas*. Classically eaten with milk or hot chocolate in the late afternoon and early evening.

Pane carasau (Sardinia): A crisp thin leavened flatbread, usually round, but sometimes rectangular, now made with fine semolina flour and usually yeasted, though until recently there was a strong domestic Sardinian sourdough tradition. This is a twice-baked bread. On first baking, the bread puffs up in a ball, like pitta or chapatti. It is then removed from the oven and when still hot the two sides are cut apart and each side re-baked, removed from the oven, and dried in stacks under weight.

Pane sciocco or Pane Toscano (Italy Regional): This is the best known modern saltless white bread. Usually with a crisp crust, it is produced in many shapes.

Panettone (Italy/International): A sweet yeasted bread that verges on cake. It is mixed with raisins and dried fruits and is traditionally eaten at Christmas.

Poppadum (India/International): A thin crispy flatbread made from a variety of non-grain starches such as lentil, chickpea, rice or potato. The raw but dried dough is fried to produce the finished bread. It is used more as a cracker than a staple food.

Paratha (Northern India and adjacent regions/International): A flatbread the size of a chapatti or roti but made by repeatedly rolling out the dough, brushing with ghee, folding and rolling again to form a type of puff pastry. In East Africa a version of the paratha is sold in restaurants under the name chapatti. There are dozens of common versions of this bread, each characterized by different flavourings or ingredients, for example, *makka paratha* (corn), *adraki mirchi paratha* (fresh ginger and fresh chilli pepper).

Parker House roll (American): The quintessential twentieth-century American milk roll. A white roll made with milk, butter and a little sugar. These rolls are increasingly rare but still served. The roll is usually cut in a small disc as for an American biscuit, pressed in the centre with a knife handle to form a depression, brushed with butter, folded in half and baked. They open slightly in the oven.

Petit pain (French): Literally 'small bread'. A common name for a roll in France. Often made with baguette dough.

Pitta (Middle East/International): The Western term for *khubz*, 'bread' in Arabic. In its international 'pitta' form it is a flat wheat bread often about 15–16 cm (6–6½ in) in diameter, usually leavened with yeast and baked in a hot oven so the two sides separate to form a hollow interior. When cooled, this pocket is often filled with fried chickpea batter to create the sandwich called falafel, an affection for which is one of the few things that both Israelis and Palestinians have in common. Similar flatbreads exist in many regions and go by local names.

Pretzel see **Brezel**

Prosphoro (Greek Orthodox/International: Yeast or sourdough leavened bread made by members of the Orthodox congregation for use in the Sunday service. Each bread is composed of two breads stuck together, with the topmost bread stamped with a seal, often hand carved and thus unique to each member of the congregation.

Pullman loaf (American): The standard American white sandwich bread. Similar to the French *pain de mie* but baked in an open tin and with a little sugar in the dough.

Pumpernickel (German/International): An old German bread from Westphalia. Historically a bread of the poor made with coarse rye meal fermented and then baked in long wooden boxes covered on four sides in a very slow oven for 24 to 48 hours. The Maillard reaction turns the bread black. A modern industrial version is widely sold internationally. It is a dense square bread that often includes whole grains and is sold packaged and pre-sliced for use in the context of a course of hors d' oeuvres. It is rarely as black as its historical antecedent. In America, pumpernickel is similar to, or even identical with American dark rye, bread that is a mix of rye and wheat, but without the caraway seeds and often darkened with the addition of caramel, coffee or cocoa.

Puri (Northern India and adjacent regions): Dough and shape similar to chapatti (often wholewheat flour, or nearly so), this bread is fried in ghee (clarified butter) or vegetable oil.

Roggenbrot (German): Rye bread made with 100 per cent rye flour. Always a sourdough bread. There are many forms, including many rustic forms with dramatically cracked top crusts. If the name includes '*volkorn*' (wholegrain) then it is a wholegrain rye.

Roggenmischbrot (German): A maslin mix with rye being dominant, what the French used to call *grand meteil*. The origin of American 'dark rye'.

Rosinenbrötchen (German): A raisin roll that is often, but not always white.

Roti (India/International): See chapatti. They can be indistinguishable to an outside observer. Roti in private homes is usually baked on the convex side of a griddle called a *tava*.

Russian black bread (US, UK/International): A *bâtard* or *boule*-shaped 100 per cent rye bread is often thought of, outside Russia and the rye belt of northern Europe, as 'Russian rye'. It is sour-leavened and made of only rye flour, water and salt. It can be made with cold water or with water just off the boil, as in the French *pain bouilli*.

Rye, light, dark and Jewish (American): Often associated with Jewish American culture, these forms of rye bread are common sandwich breads. They are usually flavoured with caraway seeds. Within a Jewish delicatessen these breads are referred to as 'light' or 'dark' rye. Outside a Jewish context the light rye is often referred to as 'Jewish rye'. The dark rye may also be made with mostly white flour. It is darkened through the use of colouring agents such as caramel, coffee or cocoa.

San Francisco sourdough (American/International): A white loaf made with a sourdough starter, usually baked in the form of a *boule*, usually around 500 g –1 kg (17 oz–2½ lb). The style is for a pronounced, even sharp, sour taste. The sourness of this bread is achieved by mixing the dough with a relatively large proportion of mature starter.

Sandwich bread (British): The standard white sandwich loaf. The loaf might be lightly enriched with milk, perhaps some fat, and include a little sugar.

Schnittbrötchen or **Schrippen (German):** The classic roll, usually *bâtard* shaped, with a deep slash down the middle. Usually made with white flour but sometimes also brown.

Scottish bap (Scottish/British): A lightly enriched milk roll.

Sesambrötchen (German): Sesame seed roll. Often similar to the *Mohnbrötchen*, poppy seed roll.

Shrak (Bedouin/Middle East): A large unleavened wholewheat bread baked on a griddle over a live fire and then used as the base on which the meal is served, similar to the Ethiopian use of *ingera*.

Siegle (French): Rye bread. Most French rye flour is pre-mixed with wheat gluten, thus today most French rye breads include at least some wheat flour. The French tend not to like breads with a sour taste, so a 100 per cent rye with a pronounced sour flavour is rarely encountered in a French bakery.

Soda bread (Irish/International): A bread that takes its name from the leavening agent, soda. It is a quick bread in the savoury bread tradition. Soda breads are traditionally cooked in a covered iron pot in front of a peat fire with the pot heated with peat underneath the pot and on the lid. Any kind of wheat flour is appropriate. Now mostly baked in modern ovens.

Sonnenblumenkernbrot (German): Sunflower seed bread. Usually a *Mehrkornbrot* (multi-grain) or *mischbrot* (rye wheat mix) with sunflower seeds in the dough and on the exterior.

Tandoori chapatti or roti (Northern India and adjacent regions/International): A chapatti or roti that has been baked on the side of a tandoor oven. A common name for these often interchangeable flatbreads in Indian restaurants.

Toastbrot (German): The classic British white sandwich loaf. Its primary function, to become toast, is implicit in the name.

Tortilla, corn (Mexico/International): A thin flatbread baked on a griddle. It is made from a paste of corn called *masa*. Masa is made from *nixtamal*, which is the name given to dried corn after it has been boiled in culinary lime, allowed to soak for many hours and then been washed clean.

Tortilla, flour (Mexico/International): A more modern form of the tortilla is one made with white flour, usually leavened with a little baking powder and softened with a small amount of lard or oil. Almost always a larger diameter than the corn tortilla. In the US this is the tortilla used to make burritos.

Vollkornbaguette (German/International): Wholegrain baguette. Increasingly fashionable in Paris, and in the US and UK, a style more associated with purveyors of 'natural food'.

Vollkornbrot (German): Wholegrain or wholemeal bread. This can thus refer to bread made with a single grain, like wheat, or to a mix of grains such as wheat, rye and barley. In German the name of the grain referred to will usually be added to the name (for example, *Roggenvollkornbrot* for rye).

Vollkornbrötchen (German): The class of wholegrain (or at least brown) rolls, usually with seeds on the top, ranging from oats to sunflowers to aromatic caraway.

Vollkornschrot (German): A coarse (*schrot*) wholegrain flour. You will sometimes find this combined with a grain such as *roggen* (rye) to describe a rustic bread.

Weizenmischbrot (German): Mixed-grain wheat/rye bread with wheat being dominant. The origin of American 'light rye'.

Wholemeal bread (British): Similar to brown bread but in this case it must be made with 100% wholemeal flour and not just brown in colour.

Wholewheat bread (American): As the name implies, made with wholewheat flour. However, it is possible that a small percentage of the largest pieces of bran have been removed. Usually sold as a sandwich bread. There could be a small amount of sugar in the dough.

Zwiebelbrot (German): Onion bread. A popular loaf bread with onions mixed into the dough.

Select Bibliography

Ashton, John, *The History of Bread from Pre-historic to Modern Times* (London, 1904)

Assire, Jérôme, *The Book of Bread* (London, 1996)

Bonnefons, Nicolas de, *Les delices de la campagne*, 2nd edn (Amsterdam, 1655)

Bottéro, Jean, *The Oldest Cuisine in the World: Cooking in Mesopotamia* (Chicago, IL, 2004)

Camporesi, Piero, *Bread of Dreams: Food and Fantasy in Early Modern Europe* (Cambridge, 1989)

Dalby, Andrew, *Empire of Pleasures: Luxury and Indulgence in the Roman World* (London and New York, 2000)

David, Elizabeth, *English Bread and Yeast Cookery* (New York, 1980)

Dupaigne, Bernard, *The History of Bread* (New York, 1999)

—, Georgette Soustelle, Monique de Fontanès, Jacques Barrau and Jean Marquis, *Le Pain* (Paris, 1979)

Estienne, Charles, *Maison rustique, or, The countrey farme*, trans. Richard Surflet, ed. Gervase Markham (London, 1616)

Husson, Camille, *Histoire du pain à toutes les époques et chez tous les peuples* (Tours, 1887)

Jacob, Heinrich Eduard, *Six Thousand Years of Bread: Its Holy and Unholy History* (New York, 1997)

Maget, Marcel, *Le pain anniversaire à Villard d'Arène en Oisans* (Paris, 1989)

Markham, Gervase, *Country Contentments: or, The Husbandmans*

Recreations & The English Housewife (London, 1615)

Parmentier, Antoine Augustin, *Avis aux bonnes ménagéres des villes et des campagnes, sur la meilleure manière de faire leur pain* (Paris, 1777)

Websites and Associations

Bakers and Bakeries

Ciril Hitz: www.breadhitz.com
De Gustibus (UK): www.degustibus.co.uk
Poilaine (Paris): www.poilane.fr

Baking Supplies

King Arthur Flour (US/Canada): www.kingarthurflour.com
Bakery Bits (UK): www.bakerybits.co.uk
Dove Farm (UK): www.dovesfarm.co.uk

Beer and Wine Yeast (Use for baking experiments)

Brew UK (UK): www.brewuk.co.uk
Seven Bridges Cooperative (US/Canada):
www.breworganic.com

Serious Amateur Bread Sites

The Fresh Loaf: www.thefreshloaf.com
Sourdough Companion: www.artisanbaker.org

Professional Organizations

Bread Bakers Guild of America: www.bbga.org
National Association of Master Bakers (UK):
www.masterbakers.co.uk
The Association of Scottish Bakers:
www.samb.co.uk

Traditional Bread Ovens

www.traditionaloven.com
Le Panyol: www.lepanyol.com

Acknowledgements

Jane Levi was both the friend who patiently listened to yet another something about bread long after it was time for me to have moved on to a different subject and also the skilful editor who helped me shape the manuscript into a publishable book.

Ancient breads are a specialist's field and I sometimes felt out of my depth. I cannot thank Delwen Samuel enough for her help with the first chapter. We had never met when I asked her to be a reader. A creative and meticulous scholar of ancient Egyptian cereals, beer and bread she unstintingly shared her knowledge with me, and with kindness and tact set me straight when she thought I'd got the story wrong. Ursula Heinzelmann provided invaluable assistance with German breads; Craig Ponsford, a master baker, read the last chapter, speculations on bread baking in the twenty-first century, and Sandy Connery, a young classics scholar, helped me with the Greek of Athaneus. As always Rachel Lauden was generous with her time and insights. I have been talking with Rachel about bread for many years; several of this book's big ideas are either hers or were inspired by conversations with her.

An astute reader, Michael Leaman, this book's publisher, sent me a challenging set of queries. The book is much better for them. While in the end I may have pressed my luck with one more deadline missed, Michael did what great publishers do, he gave the book time to become itself. My editor, Martha Jay, was a pleasure to work with. She skilfully brought that last layer of polish to the text.

Photo Acknowledgements

The author and the publishers wish to express their thanks to the below sources of illustrative material and/or permission to reproduce it.

© The Trustees of The British Museum: pp. 11, 16, 23, 24; Children's Art Foundation, Santa Cruz, California: p. 26 (Saber Hassan El Sharkawi); Chris Connery: p. 90; Istock: p. 6 (Artiom Muhaciov); Michael Leaman: p. 74; Jane Levi: p. 31; The National Library of Medicine, Maryland: p. 37; Mark Nesbitt: p. 12; Museo Archeologico, Naples: p. 35; Musée du Louvre: pp. 40, 43; William Rubel: pp. 14, 25, 29, 45, 50, 51, 53, 57, 62, 63, 66, 68, 77, 81, 83, 85, 86, 87, 88, 89, 97, 101, 107; Photo © 2011 Scala, Florence: pp. 36, 73 (The National Gallery, London); University of California, San Diego: p. 33; Werner Forman Archive: p. 28 (E. Strouhal).

Index

italic numbers refer to illustrations; **bold** to recipes

Algeria, *khobz eddar* 102
Armenia, *lavash* 102, 140
artisan bakers 82, 106–7, 112
    flours used by 62, 65, 71
    and gender 109–10
    and preservatives 78
    and technology 35, 111
    see also individual countries
ash cakes 47, 74, 133
Athenaeus, *Deipnosophistae* 32–3, 35, 39

bagel 133
baguette 43, 67, 87, 98, 99, 134
    crumb texture range *62, 63,* 64
Balkans, *lepinja* 51
barley bread 13, 23, 28, 32–3, 35, *47*
batter breads 8, 35, 74, **123–4**
    see also ciabatta
Baugin, Lubin, *Still-life with Chessboard* 40, *40,* 65, 129
Bayes, Alfred, *Baking Oatcakes, Britain 48*
beer and wine yeasts 17–18, 24, 29, 73, 115–16, 120–21
    see also yeast leavening
Best, Henry, *Memorandum Book 45,* 46, 54, 124

Beuckelaer, Joachim, *The Four Elements: Air 73*
black bread 53, 91, 93, 144, 145
blinis 51, *51,* 134
Bonnefons, Nicolas de, *Les Delices de la compaigne* 54–5, 84
    pain à la Montoron **54**
Bottero, Jean 24–5
bread
    concept of and use of term 7–9
    first appearance of 10
    forms and shapes, early 19–20
    freshness 67
    machine, domestic 111
    nutritional components 41, 52
    ovens 35, *56,* 75, *88,* 102, *107, 120,* 121
    staling 67, 68–9
    see also crumb; flavour factors; grains; individual bread types and countries; leavening
Brontë, Charlotte, *Shirley* 49
brown bread, early 44, 45–6, *45,* 124, 136

Cambodia, *petit pain* 80, 81
campfire bread 18–19, 22, **121–2**

Chardin, Jean-Baptiste-Siméon,
  Return from the Market 56–7
Charpentier, Henri 51–2
Child, Julia 98
China, Shanghai bakery *90*
chipped and rasped bread 66–7,
  131–2
Christianity
  bread, and body of Christ 38,
    138–9, 144
  saints and coarse bread 33, *33*
ciabatta 35, 64, 94, 99, 137
Cogan, Thomas 36, 60–62
Cotgrave, Randall 71–2
crêpes 8, 51–2
crumb, light 60–64, *63*
crust
  and baking stone 121
  and bread style 65–6, *66*
  brown, and salt 72
  chipped and rasped bread
    66–7, **131–2**
  and French bread 86
  and freshness 69
  health problems associated
    with 66–7, 131

David, Elizabeth 22
Dickens, Charles 141
  Dombey and Son 41
Diderot, 'The Threshing Floor'
  13
dinner roll 30–31

Egypt
  Baking Bread at Home 26
  flatbreads 100
Egypt, ancient
  blood bread 30
  bread-related artefacts 27–8
  grains used in 28–9
  hieroglyphics, bread in 30

Nebhepetre Mentuhotep II
  tomb *16*
  Qenamun tomb *28*
  sourdough 17, 29
  tomb bread, Deir el-Bahari,
    Thebes 29–30, *29*
Ellis, William 52–3
Ethiopia, *ingera* 8, 139, 146
Europe
  bread hierarchy 47–9
  see also individual countries;
    Roman Europe

Farmer, Fanny 131, 132
Fertile Crescent
  bread types 18–19
  and early bread 10–13
  grindstones 14–15, *14, 16*
  urbanization 22–5
  see also Egypt, Ancient; Iraq,
    Ancient
flatbreads
  ash cakes 47, 74, 133
  baking methods 75
  barley *47*
  leavening 17, 73, 74
  pulse flour **123–4**
  regions 100–101
  and sourdough 52
  thick 102–3
  unleavened 9, 74, **121–2**
flavour factors 70, 75, 120
Fleishmann's Recipes 61
flour *see* grains
France
  artisan breads 82–7, *85, 86*
  bâtard 134
  boule 135, 141, 142
  bread oven, Villar d'Arène
    68
  brioche 43, 55, 135
  chickpea flatbread (*socca*) 123

crêpes 8, 51–2
croissant 137
crusts, nearly burnt (*bien cuit*) 65
ficelle 87, 138
fougasse 85, 138
levain (sourdough) leavening
  76–7, 78, 86–7
maslin (*meteil*) bread **127–8**,
  140
mechanical kneader *105*
milling *84*, *106*
pain à la Montoron **54**, 76,
  130–31
pain à la Reine 54, 76
pain à l'ancienne 86–7, 141
pain bouilli 57, 68, 142
pain de campagne 43, 71, 99, 105,
  106–7, 135, 142
pain de mie **130–31**, 132, 142
petit pain 87, 144
Poilâne bakery, Paris 35, 67,
  70–1
siegle (rye bread) **127**, 146
sugar, lack of, in bread 70–71
white bread consumption 42
yeast leavening, injunction
  against 76–7
French bread, English 41, **55**

Galen 36, 76
gender 109–10
Germany
  artisan breads 90–91
  Brötchen 136, 145, 146
  home-grown bread traditions
    91–2
  Life Reform Movement 92
  Mehrkornbrot 140
  pretzels (Brezel) 135, 136, 144
  rye breads 91–2, 95, 141, 145,
    147
  seeded breads 91, 139, 140, 141,
    147
  Toastbrot 147
  Westphalian pumpernickel
    bread 52–3, 91, 144
  wholegrain breads 147–8
  Zwiebelbrot (onion bread) 148
Graham, Sylvester 138
grains
  and archaeological research
    11–13, *12*, 32
  einkorn *12*, 13, 15–16
  grinding 14–15, *14*, 122
  and modern flour production
    108, 119–20
  pulse flour *see* pulse flour
  threshing 13–14, *13*
  wheat, preference for, in
    Ancient Greece 36–8
  wheat prices, and size of loaf
    46–7
  wild emmer 13, 28, 32
Greece
  prosphoro 144
  yufka, Cappadocia 51
Greece, ancient
  bread in the arts 30–31, *31*
  bread types 31–3
  flour and bread classifications
    36–8
  flour grinding 122
  white bread 36–8
Guercino, *St Paul the Hermit 33*

Harrison, William 110
Herp, Willem van, *St Anthony . . .*
  Distributing Bread 36
home bread-making, modern 107
Homer, *Odyssey* 30
horse-bread 43–4, 45, *45*, **125–6**
Houghton, John 126
Howard, William, 'French bread'
  55–6

Iceland, *Laufabrauð 74*, 139
India
    flatbreads 74, 100–103, **122**,
        123, 136, 141, 143, 145, 147
    flour grinding 122
industrial bakeries 112–14, 117
Iraq, ancient
    bread moulds 26–7
    cuneiform tablets *11, 24*
    farming and centralized irriga-
        tion 22–3
    milling rooms, Ebla 24–6
    Panel of Ashurnasirpal *25*, 26–7
    tandoor-style ovens 25–6
    Uruk, and Epic of Gilgamesh
        23–4, *23*, 25
Ireland, soda bread 73, 146
Italy
    ciabatta 35, 64, 94, 99, 137
    flatbreads 49–51, 123, **124**
    pane di Altamura, Apulia 34
    panettone 143
    piadina 49–50
    Pompeii *34*, 35
    tigelle and *crescentine* 49
    torta di ceci flatbread 123, **124**
    Tuscany saltless bread 72, 143

Jewish
    challah 99, 136
    matzo 74, 140
    rye bread 99, 145
Johnson, Samuel 48–9

Kazakhstan, *taba-nan* 103
Kenya, industrial breads *81*
kneaded dough 8, *28, 105*

Le Nain, Louis, *The Happy Family*
    40, *43*
leavening 17, 72–4
    rye bread 126

steam 17, 72, 73, 74, 75, 121
    see also sourdough; yeast
    leavening
levain see sourdough
Liger, Louis, *Maison rustique* 130–31
Lithuania
    blinis *51*, 134
    mouldy bread 69
    rye breads 96–7
loaf breads 17, 73, 75, 81, 82
    adulterated with pulse flours
        124–5
    pain de mie **130–31**, 132, 142
    sugar in 70–71, 110

McGee, Harold, *On Food and
    Cooking* 67
Maget, Marcel 127
Maison rustique, or, the Countrey Farme
    54–5, 66–7
Malouin, Paul-Jacques 71, 77
manchet 36, 64, **128–30**
Markham, Gervase, *The English
    Housewife* 44, 45, 124, 129–30
maslin bread **127–8**, 140
Mexico
    artisan breads 87–90, *87, 89*
    bolillo (savoury rolls) 88, 135
    bread ovens *88, 120*
    concha 88, 137
    mantecato 89
    milk bread *89*
    pan dulce 88, 96, 137, 142
    panadería (wheat bread) 7
    tortillas 7, 14–15, 147
Meydenbach, J., *Hortus Sanitatis 37*
Middle East
    manakish 140
    shrak 146
Millet, Jean-François, *Les Glaneuses*
    47
mixing containers 120

Morocco, *khobz* 139
mouldy bread 69, 78

Neolithic Revolution 21–2

oatcakes *48*, 48–9
organic flour 78–9

pain à la Montoron **54, 130–31**
pain de mie **130–31**, 132, 142
pancakes *see* batter breads
Parmentier, Augustin 71, 77, 105
petit pain 80, 81, 87, 144
Piperno, Dolores 12–13
pitta bread 74, 144
Poilâne, Lionel 35, 67, 71
Poland, rye bread 93
Pope, Alexander 38
Portugal, *broa* 136
pulse flour
    chickpea flatbread **123–4**
    loaf bread adulterated with
    124–5

Rajasthan, flour milling 22
Randolph, Mary, *The Virginia Housewife* 131
Roman Europe 33–5, *34*, 36
Romania 107, *107*
    crêpes *51*
Rousseau, Jean-Jacques 20
Russia
    artisan breads 92–3
    black rye breads 42, 93, 145
    blinis 51, 134
    bread price controls 93
rye bread 35, 42, 91, 93, 96–7, 99,
    126–7, 145
    adulterated **124–5**
    crust *66*
    leavening 126
    Pain bouilli 57, 68, 142

    with pattern *53*
    rehydrated 69
    slicing, delaying 67
    and sourdough 78
    sticky crumb 61

salt
    as flavour 71–2
    saltless bread 72, 80, 81
Samuel, Delwen 17, 30
Sardinia
    Easter bread 19
    pane carasau 50–51, *50*, 143
Scandinavia cracker-breads 49, 74,
    139
Sloan's Cook Book 110
social marker
    bread at modern table 58
    white bread, consumption by
    elites 16–17, 36–43, 47–8, 53–5,
    56, 62–3
sourdough 17, 18, 73, 77–8
    and chewy crumb 64
    and flatbreads 50–51, 52, 74
    health factors 76
    and horse-bread 44, 45, *45*,
    125–6
    sour flavour, changing attitudes
    to 71
Spain, Pan Picado *77*
staling 67, 68–9
steam leavening 17, 72, 73, 74, 75,
    121
sugar in yeasted loaf breads 70–71,
    110
Sweden, *knäckebröd* 49, 139

Tasahara Bread Book 70–71
toasting 67–8, 95–6
torta di ceci flatbread **124**
tortillas 7, 15, 147
Tyron, Thomas 36

UK
artisan breads 93–4
barley bread 134
bloomer and cottage loaf 94,
134, 137
bread laws 44, 46–7
brown bread, early 44, 45–6, *45*,
124, 135
cheat bread 136
crumpets 138
flatbreads *48*, 49, 53, **123–4**,
134, 141
French bread 41, **55**
horse-bread 43–4, 45, *45*, **125–6**
industrial bread 94, 146
manchet 36, 63, **128–30**
maslin bread **127–8**, 140
muffins 141
oatcakes *48*, 49
poverty and industrialization
57–8
Scottish bap 146
sugar in yeasted loaf breads 70
tinned breads 95
toast 67–8, 95–6
wholemeal bread 148
US
artisan breads 96–9, *101*
Boston brown bread 135
cornbread 137
Francophile bakeries 98–9, *101*
French roll 138
fry bread 138
Graham bread 138
griddle breads *50*
hamburger bun 80
hippie bakeries 98
industrial bread 96, 99
Jewish immigrant breads 99,
145
Parker House roll 143
Pullman loaf 144

pumpernickel bread 144
Quotidian Bakery, NYC *83*
sourdough breads 99, 146
sugar in yeasted loaf breads 70,
81
tinned breads 97
wholewheat bread 138, 148
Wonder Bread *113*

Vine, Frederick 59

'Warner's Safe Yeast' *76*
white bread
colour and flavour 65, 70
consumption by elites 16–17,
36–43, 47–8, 53–4, 56
fats, addition of 54–5
lightness, and status 53–5, 62–3
mass-produced 42, 55, 56,
59–60
milling process 15–17
pain à la Montoron **54–5**
pain de mie **130–31**, 132, 142
slicing, delaying 67
wholegrain bread 43, 91, 120, 138,
147–8
hippie bakeries 98
and light crumb 62
and nutrition 53

yeast leavening 75–6
beer and wine yeasts 17–18, 24,
29, 73, 115–16, 120–21
dried yeast 121
flavour and modern research
115–17
and health factors 76–7
and lightness of bread 54–5
sugar in yeasted loaf breads
70–71, 110
see also leavening; sourdough